AN INTRODUCT

ANTHROPOS

By the same author:

*An Introduction to Steiner Education, The Waldorf School*

# AN INTRODUCTION TO
# ANTHROPOSOPHY

## Rudolf Steiner's World View

## Francis Edmunds

Sophia Books

Sophia Books
Hillside House, The Square
Forest Row, RH18 5ES

www.rudolfsteinerpress.com

Published by Sophia Books 2005
An imprint of Rudolf Steiner Press

First published under the title *Anthroposophy, A Way of Life* by Carnant
Books in 1982. This edition has been edited, revised and updated by
Matthew Barton

A catalogue record for this book is available from the British Library

ISBN 1 85584 163 0

Cover by Andrew Morgan Design
Typeset by DP Photosetting, Aylesbury, Bucks.
Printed and bound in Great Britain by 4edge Limited

# CONTENTS

# FOREWORD

It is not easy to find a compact but comprehensive introduction to the life and work of Rudolf Steiner. Many of his works are still untranslated or are out of print. And while there is now an extensive secondary literature in German, there is less in English.

This may be partly because those who have encountered Steiner's work in the English-speaking world have been fired to undertake all kinds of activities which have left them little time to write. In recent years, Waldorf schools (which derive from the new school pioneered with Steiner's help in Stuttgart in 1919) have been founded all over the world, as have new homes and communities for children and adults with special needs. The new work in medicine, agriculture, architecture, the arts, and even banking, which has developed strongly in continental Europe, is also beginning to be better known in England, the United States and many other parts of the world. The prophetic quality of Steiner's thought, and the creative potential in the path he called anthroposophy, are becoming ever more apparent in our times.

So a work of this kind, which is both a survey of Steiner's extraordinary achievement and a personal testimony, is of great value. It comes from a man whose life was fired and guided by Steiner's work, and who played a major part in bringing his impulses for education to life.

From his youth, Francis Edmunds lived as a practical idealist. As a medical student, a relief worker in Russia, then as a teacher, he saw with passion and compassion that the ills of the world are rooted in a crippled understanding of human nature. The scientific age tries to persuade us that we are fundamentally machines or animals, and so it is blind to the possibility that we may also be angels-in-the-making. Life shapes itself accordingly.

Impelled by a sense of human life as a journey of the spirit to discover and realize its true nature, on encountering Steiner's work Francis Edmunds could see instantly that it contained both the vision and the path for which he had been searching. After the First World War he began teaching, first at the Friends' School in Lebanon for three years, and then at the International School in Geneva for two years before joining the first English Waldorf School in Streatham, London, in 1932.

He and a group of gifted colleagues carried this school through the Second World War, relocating it to its present home in Forest Row, Sussex. In the 1950s he began to visit the United States and help the developing Waldorf school movement there, inspiring parents, teachers and children alike. This activity he later extended to South Africa, Australia, New Zealand and Brazil.

During the second world war he was increasingly pre-occupied with questions of adult education. The impulse being realized in the Waldorf schools needed its continuation into further and higher education. The universities and colleges of the Western world are often citadels of that crippled view of nature and human nature which obscures the living creative spirit in both. How could adult centres for education and training develop which, as he later put it, spring from 'a concept of the human being which can imbue life with grace, purpose and meaning'?

While in the United States, Francis Edmunds had come to recognize in the works of Ralph Waldo Emerson a nineteenth-century spirit striving towards the ideals that Steiner began to realize in the twentieth. In 1962, when he came to found a new centre for adult education with the help of a group of English and American friends, he chose for it the name Emerson College. In the years following, he devoted his main energies to building up this College, which began in connection with Sunfield Children's Homes at Clent, and then moved to Forest Row in order to collaborate with Michael Hall school in teacher training. The College has now added to its original 'foundation year' a wide variety of short and further training courses in fields ranging from agriculture to the arts and education, and draws students from all over the world.

Francis Edmunds continued to travel widely, lecturing, teaching, supporting and encouraging new pioneering ventures born out of anthroposophy. Thus what he presents in this book has been not only thought but lived. For the true idealist, ideals are not simply attractive thoughts to be contemplated at one remove from reality, but are truths to be sought, found and realized in life itself. So this guide to Steiner's work has been engendered, as Steiner himself would certainly have wished it, not out of theory but out of a life lived to the full.

JOHN DAVY
1982

# PREFACE

A word about the author and what led to this book.

As a youth at college during the First World War, two questions weighed on me. The one concerned science, the other life.

How could we have evolved a science which reduces the human being to a creature of chance, a nonentity? How could a society claiming to be advanced and based on reason find itself plunged into a war more murderously destructive than any in known history? Science seemed meaningless and life an intolerable contradiction. Where was truth?

Long pondering led me to realize that the truth I sought could only be born from within. Was that what was meant by acquiring other eyes and ears? Was that the meaning of the second birth? How could one attain it? I set out to find a way not based on past faiths and traditions but arising from my own explorations and experience.

Someone at this time brought me a book and asked me for my opinion. I found the title off-putting. It suggested the book had something to tell but I was set on finding my own way. Nevertheless I felt obliged to read it. Having begun I did not put it down again until the last page. The book was *Knowledge of Higher Worlds* by Rudolf Steiner.

Every word in the book seemed weighed and tested in the strictest sense of any science I knew, and every sentence breathed of a new life to be discovered.

All this was long ago. Now, in advanced old age, a friend still older than myself for whom I have the highest regard unexpectedly asked me to write an introduction to anthroposophy to meet a growing need. It came at that moment as a challenge and this small book is an attempt, however inadequate, to meet it.

As the writing proceeded it seemed to take over and develop naturally into its present form. Wherever it was a question of how Rudolf Steiner himself stood in regard to his work, especially in the early stages, it seemed best to quote him directly, as a way also for the reader to make a more immediate connection with him.

The word 'anthroposophy' dates back to 1742 or possibly earlier. Composed of the words *anthropos* and *sophia* the Oxford Dictionary gives its meaning as 'knowledge of the nature of man' or simply as 'human wisdom'. Rudolf Steiner adopted the word as closest to his needs. The word is no more than a signpost; he would have preferred a new word each day.

It is hoped that the anthroposophy presented here may serve as a living force in its bearing on the times we live in, and in a modest way as a guide for further study and for inner and outer work.

FRANCIS EDMUNDS
1982

# 1
# THE WAY OF RUDOLF STEINER
(based on his *Autobiography*)

There have been great spiritual teachers throughout the ages. There could be no discord among them for they drew their wisdom from a single source. Yet each had to frame his teaching according to the needs of his time and this is true also of Rudolf Steiner. He was born into an age of acute scepticism in regard to spiritual matters. Materialistic thinking dominated, as it still does in schools, informing and determining the practical conduct of life. We are fortunate to have his autobiography (written at the request of others) to help us to understand better the kind of man he was and the trials he had to go through. This chapter relates particularly to his life and work in the nineteenth century to prepare for his teaching of anthroposophy in the twentieth.

## *The early years*

As a quite young child, Steiner had to learn that he was understood when he spoke of certain things, but not when he spoke of others. He carried a world within him from which those around him were excluded. He could enter their world but they could not enter his. Even before the age of eight he had learnt to distinguish between 'a world seen' and 'a world not seen'. This imposed on him a silence and great loneliness.

In the eyes of others he was a healthy, normal child, helpful in the home and able at school. He was not a dreamer; on the contrary, he was very attentive to the people he met and to what was going on around him. There was always one or

another adult who inclined warmly towards him, but there
was nothing about him, even in his parents' eyes, to mark him
out as being quite exceptional.

At about the age of ten an event occurred unperceived by
others, but for him decisive. He saw on the bookshelf of the
assistant master of the school he was then attending a book
on geometry, and was allowed to borrow it. It was a new
subject to him. He describes how he plunged into it with
enthusiasm. For weeks on end his mind was filled with 'the
coincidence, the similarity of triangles, squares, polygons'. He
racked his brains over the question 'where do parallel lines
meet?' The theorem of Pythagoras fascinated him. Geometry
came to him as a revelation.

> That one can live within the mind in the shaping of forms
> perceived only within oneself, entirely without impression
> upon the external senses, became for me the deepest satis-
> faction. I found in this a solace for the unhappiness which
> my unanswered questions had caused me. To be able to lay
> hold upon something in the spirit alone brought me an
> inner joy. I am sure that I learned through geometry to
> know happiness for the first time.

Joy and happiness are strong terms. Perhaps there was a
dawning sense, which could scarcely have been formulated at
the time, that there might after all be the possibility of communicating about a world 'not seen', and being understood.
The above description was written in retrospect very late in
Rudolf Steiner's life. He then adds, 'I should have been forced
to feel the physical world as a sort of spiritual darkness if it
had not received light from that side,' that is from that inner
world in which he 'loved to live'.

One can sense this as an early premonition of his future
task. Without that light, humanity was living in a state of

spiritual darkness, threatened as a consequence with rapid decline. Pure thinking, that is thinking not bound to the senses but as exercised in geometry, provided him with a ground on which to proceed further. The 'joy' was one of relief and release.

> In my relation to geometry I perceived the first budding of a conception which later gradually evolved within me. This lived within me more or less unconsciously during my childhood, and about my twentieth year took a definite and fully conscious form. I said to myself: 'The objects and occurrences which the senses perceive are in space. But, just as this space is outside man, so there exists within man a sort of soul-space which is the scene of action of spiritual beings and occurrences.' I could not look upon thoughts as something like images which the human being forms of things; on the contrary, I saw in them revelations of a spiritual world on this field of action in the soul ... for the reality of the spiritual world was to me as certain as that of the physical. I felt the need, however, for a sort of justification of this assumption. I wished to be able to say to myself that the experience of the spiritual world is just as little an illusion as is that of the physical world. With regard to geometry, I said to myself: 'Here one is *permitted* to know something which the mind alone through its own power experiences.' In this feeling I found the justification for speaking of the spiritual world that I experienced as no less real than the physical.

In geometry we exercise sense-free thinking. The senses can stimulate our thinking but thinking itself is freeborn within us. Once this distinction is made, it follows that it should be possible to grasp in pure thought the facts of higher knowledge presented by someone endowed with spiritual perception. It is to this faculty of 'pure thinking' that anthroposophy addresses itself. A great part of Rudolf Steiner's labour was to translate his higher knowledge into ideas and images which the thinking mind can then grasp in all freedom and make its own.

Seeing plants does not make one a botanist, nor does having spiritual perceptions make one a spiritual investigator. Rudolf Steiner has aptly been described as *A Scientist of the Invisible*, the title of a book about him by Canon A. P. Shepherd. He was an arduous worker. His formal training was in mathematics and science but he himself extended this to philosophy and the classics, all the time relating his outer studies to his inner life and vice versa. He made it his special task to bridge the abyss in modern life between inner and outer.

I felt duty bound at that time to seek for the truth through philosophy. I had to study mathematics and science. I was convinced that I should find no relation with them unless I could place their findings on a solid foundation of philosophy. But I beheld a spiritual world *as reality*. In perfectly clear vision the spiritual individuality of everyone was manifest to me. This came to expression in the physical body and in action in the physical world. It united itself with the physical germ derived from a person's parents. After death I could follow a human being on his way into the spiritual world. After the death of a schoolmate I wrote about this phase of my spiritual life to one of my former teachers who had continued to be a close friend of mine after my High School days. He wrote back to me with unusual affection, but he did not deign to say one word about what I had written regarding the dead schoolmate. But this is what happened to me always at that time in relation to my perceptions of the spiritual world . . . No one would pay any attention to it.

There was one exception to this in the guise of 'a simple man of the people', a herb gatherer who sold his medicinal plants to the Vienna apothecaries.

With him, it was possible to look deep into the mysteries of nature. He carried on his back the bundle of medicinal plants, but in his heart he bore the discoveries which he had won from the spirituality of nature through gathering herbs.

This figure appears in the character of Felix Balde in Rudolf Steiner's *Four Mystery Dramas*, written many years later.

Such people are still to be met, though usually in remote places. The author met such a man at the centre of a Shetland island. I had gone to see a Druid circle there. Close by was a long single-storied building called a blackhouse, divided one half for the family and the other for their animals. It was there he lived. There was a natural nobility about him. His blue eyes had an inward look. In the course of conversation he said, 'We old ones have our regular meetings in order to keep alive the old wisdom,' and later, rather sadly, 'Our children go to school and learn reading and writing, and laugh at what we know.' In him and his ageing companions there were still 'souls which see'. They bore witness to a kind of vision and seeing which preceded the modern life of thought. The time has come for our thinking to grow to a new art of seeing. That is what anthroposophy is about.

The life of thought came gradually to seem to me the reflection radiated into the physical human being out of what the soul experiences in the spiritual world. Thought experience was for me existence in a reality—as something actually experienced through and through—there was no room for doubt. The world of the senses did not seem to me so completely a matter of experience. It is present but one does not lay hold upon it as upon thought. Yet the human being himself is set in the midst of this world. Then the question arose: Is *this* world, then, a reality complete in itself? When, in relation to it, the human being weaves thoughts out of his inner being, which bring light into the world of the senses, is he actually bringing into this world something which is foreign to it? This certainly does not accord with the experience that we have when we engage with the world of the senses and penetrate it by means of our thoughts. Thought, then, surely appears to be that by means of which the world of the senses experiences *its own nature*. The further development of this reflection was at that time an important part of my inner life.

That we are able in some degree to enter into Rudolf Steiner's own struggles to attain the clarity he sought on such fundamental issues comes to us as a very special gift through his *Autobiography*. For example, even whilst at High School, out of his scant earnings from coaching fellow students he scraped together enough to purchase a copy of Kant's *Critique of Pure Reason*. Kant was then considered supreme amongst philosophers. He subscribed to the eighteenth-century slogan 'mathematics is the key to the universe', a mathematics which underlay the mechanistic-materialistic view of the universe whilst at the same time maintaining his belief in a moral world order. Thus the world was split into two irreconcilable halves, a view which was in direct contradiction to Rudolf Steiner's experience.

How was it possible to relate to a world held in movement

by the dead laws of inertia through endless space and time? At this point help came again from geometry and the new concepts arising from it.

A decisive experience came to me at that time precisely from the direction of mathematics. The conception of space gave me the greatest inner difficulty. As the illimitable, all-encompassing void—the form upon which the dominant theories of contemporary science were based—it could not be conceived in any definite manner. Through the more recent (synthetic) geometry which I learned through lectures and through private study, there came into my mind the perception that a line prolonged infinitely towards the right would return again from the left to its starting point. The infinitely distant point on the right is the same as the infinitely distant point on the left... The straight line returning on itself like a curve seemed to me to be a revelation. I left the lecture at which this had first passed through my mind as if a great load had fallen from me. A feeling of liberation came over me again, as in early boyhood, something joy-bestowing had come to me through geometry.

Immediately following this he writes:

Behind the riddle of space stood at that time in my life the riddle of time. Ought a conception to be possible there too which would contain within itself the idea of returning out of the past into the 'infinitely distant' future? My happiness about the space concept led to profound unrest about that of time. But there was no apparent way out. All effort of thought led me only to the realization that I must beware of applying a perceptible spacial concept to that of time. All the disappointments which can arise from the striving for knowledge I experienced in connection with the riddle of time.

If we take the infinite to mean what is not finite and cannot be confined to any given measure (as for instance in infinite Father, infinite love, compassion, devotion and so on) then in breaking away from the idea of mere endlessness of space and time we come a little closer to the heart of the question.

In point of fact, this problem of time led to a totally new conception of repeated earth lives: past experience transmuted in the course of its passage through the spiritual worlds through the 'infinite' morality of divine being returns newly gifted and circumstanced for shaping a new life. Past is transmuted into future. Along these lines the idea of reincarnation enters the domain of a science scarcely begun as yet, the science of metamorphosis of which Goethe was a great pioneer.

In these pages I wish to show that anthroposophy is not simply knowledge to be received but is something to be striven for. It is in promoting such inner striving that its mission lies, for in that way alone can genuine progress arise. And always it calls for clear thinking and discriminating judgement. The twentieth century has raised many questions about the nature of science and the way it is going. James Jeans in his *Physics and Philosophy* states quite baldly that much that was assumed to be objective turns out to consist of 'subjective mental constructs'. Certain values have been selected in deliberate disregard of others and theories have been constructed upon them. In *The Nature of the Physical World*, Arthur Eddington—like Jeans a prominent astrophysicist—compares the physicist's construction of the universe to a house that Jack built leaving in it no room for Jack. W. J. N. Sullivan, in his book *Limitation of Science*, writes the following:

We see that the scientific outlook, as presented by Galileo, constitutes a really amazing revolution in thought. The vivid world of the mediaevalist, a world shot through with beauty, and instinct with purpose, a world having an intimate relationship to his own destiny, and an intelligible reason for existing in the light of that destiny, is dismissed as an illusion. It has no objective existence. The real world, as revealed by science, is a world of material particles, moving in accordance with mathematical laws, through space and time.

Rudolf Steiner as a student entered deeply into the scientific theories holding sway. He was specially concerned at one time with the mechanical theory of heat and the wave theory of light.

At that time the external physical world was conceived as material processes of motion. Sensations seemed to be only subjective processes, the effects of pure motion upon the senses of the human being. Out there in space, it was assumed, occur dynamic, material processes; if these processes affect the human sense for heat, the sensation of heat is experienced. Outside of man are wave processes in ether; if these affect the optic nerve, light and colour sensations are generated. This conception met me everywhere. It caused me unspeakable difficulties in my thinking. It banished all spirit from the objective external world.

What position did he adopt in relation to this? He goes on:

Even so I could not yet resolve to set against prevailing ideas a manner of thinking of my own, even for myself alone. But this very fact caused me bitter soul struggles. Again and again the criticism I could easily formulate against this way of thinking had to be suppressed within me to await a time when more comprehensive sources and ways of knowledge could give me greater assurance.

Out of his wrestling with such questions came Rudolf Steiner's doctoral thesis, *Truth and Science*, and later, his *Philosophy of Freedom*. Later still came his lecture courses on heat, on light, also on astronomy, opening up quite new modes of research. He had the highest regard for all that scientists were able to discover, but they stopped dead at the frontiers to the spirit. They had acquired an immense knowledge of outer data without entry into what lived within. This is equally true of the biological sciences. What rules in the multitudinous forms in nature, what quickens the life in plants, what wakens sense-life in the animals, what manifests as thinking spirit in man? It is to these sciences that Rudolf Steiner now turns.

I observed human, animal and plant phenomena—I became more and more aware that the picture of nature which is attainable through the senses penetrates through to what was visible to me in a spiritual way.

If in this spiritual way I directed my gaze to the soul activity of the human being, in thinking, feeling and will, the 'spiritual human being' took form for me even as a clearly visible image. I could not linger in the abstractions of which it is customary to think when speaking of think-ing, feeling and will. In these inner manifestations of life I saw creative forces which placed the 'human being as spirit' spiritually before me. If I then directed my gaze to the human being's physical embodiment, this was supple-mented to my reflective contemplation by the spiritual form which underlies sense-perception.

Concerning his further researches into this subject he wrote:

My look fell, at first in a very imperfect way, upon the threefold organization of the human being, about which—after having pursued my study of it for thirty years in silence—I first began to speak publicly in my book *Riddles of the Soul*.

This gives us a glimpse into what such work entailed, what patient labour spread over decades, before the results were ready to be shared with others. The threefold human organism becomes a master key to understanding not only the human being but the whole world related to him.

## Steiner and Goethe

A powerful factor in Rudolf Steiner's life was the work he did on Goethe, both the poet and the scientist. As a poet Goethe is universally acknowledged, as scientist hardly at all even to this day, though he himself believed his science would outlive his poetry.

As to Goethe the poet, I once found myself in the company of outstanding Goetheanists in Britain. They could not eulogize sufficiently about him as a poet and sage, but there was only one who concerned himself seriously with his science. The second part of *Faust* they found largely incomprehensible, attributing this to the fact that Goethe wrote it in his old age. It may be mentioned that the immense work of *Faust* Parts One and Two is performed at regular two-yearly intervals unexpurgated and with great artistry at the Goetheanum in Dornach near Basle, the world centre of the Anthroposophical Society. Rudolf Steiner gave many lectures on *Faust* and other literary works by Goethe. We might also mention how he felt at one time a need to meditate on the fairy tale *The Green Snake and the Beautiful Lily* and how after twenty-one years it appeared transformed in his own first mystery play, *The Portal of Initiation.*

It is for his work on Goethe the scientist that the world owes much to him, though this too has so far been little acknowledged. Some of his followers, stimulated by him, have continued research along Goetheanistic lines, but to the world at large Goethe's outlook on nature remains unfamiliar or, at best, enigmatic.

It was while Rudolf Steiner the student was preoccupied with questions of light and colour, not satisfied with the current explanations based on Newton, that he first came across Goethe's work.

We will not enter here into the controversy that has raged around the Goethean theory of colour as opposed to that of Newton. If rage is the word, then Goethe raged against Newton; and the rest of the world, with rare exceptions, raged against Goethe. We need, however, to mention briefly the contrasting circumstances, for they reflect back on the people at their centre.

Newton placed a prism in the path of a beam of white light and saw a band of colours appear on a screen. Placing another prism in reverse he saw the colours vanish again into a white beam. He concluded that the colours were already contained within the white light. On emergence they were dispersed according to their different refractive indices and then were reassembled as white light. Being the mathematician he was, he arrived at a mathematical scale to match the colours and this has served industry well, for the scale can be used to determine any shade of colour within the spectrum.

With Goethe the matter took a different course. He clapped the prism to his eye expecting to see the spectrum of which he had read. Instead he saw two bands of colour, a light and a dark one and no green between them at all. Only when the two bands were drawn together to overlap, did the green appear as a secondary effect. Goethe was greatly interested in the *qualities* of colours, and for him the primary phenomenon lay in the two contrasting bands. These he interpreted as the interplay of the forces of light and darkness. He saw darkness as an active power in the world in opposition to light. Where darkness intervenes between the eye and the object, as with the greater density of atmosphere before a sinking sun, the brightness of the sun is dimmed down to red. On the other hand where light streams in between the eye and the object, as in gazing at distant hills or at the sky, darkness is raised to blue. Goethe went so far as to describe colours as the deeds and sufferings of light—something which others regard as unwarranted fantasy.

But Goethe saw the whole of life in terms of polarity. He saw the root of the plant contracting into the earth, and the blossoms unfolding towards the open breadths of the heavens, and the leaf mediating variously between the below and the above. For Goethe light and darkness, joy and grief, elation and depression, were equally polar realities within the life of soul. So were night and day, winter and summer polarities, also outer life and the life within, each had its counterpart in the other. Life and death also expressed such a polarity, as the following lines by Goethe, often quoted by Rudolf Steiner show:

> As long as you do not grasp
> This interplay of death and birth,
> You're but an anxious guest
> Upon the gloomy earth.

The whole wondrous world of colours with all their expressiveness was dead, laid out in the spectrum. It left one blind to their living qualities. It was like robbing life of meaning. It was this that troubled Goethe so deeply.

How then did Rudolf Steiner enter into all this? Being fully familiar with the usual experiments on light and colour and also with the mathematical treatment of optics, he could say:

> In spite of all objections raised by the physicist against Goethe's theory of colour, I was driven by my own experiments further away from the customary view and towards Goethe. I said to myself that colours are not, as Newton thinks, produced out of light: they come to manifestation when obstructions hinder the free unfolding of light. But light was thus removed for me from the category of truly physical elements of reality. It presented itself as a midway stage between the realities perceptible to the senses and those visible to the spirit.
>
> I was not inclined to engage in merely philosophical processes of thinking about these things. But I laid strong emphasis upon *reading the facts of nature aright*. It then became clearer to me that light itself does *not* enter the realm of sense-perception, but remains on the farthest side of this, while colours appear when the sense-perceptible is brought into the realm of light.

We can see Newton standing in a dark room, aware of the light streaming in, but ignoring the darkness and thus concluding that the colours are produced out of the light itself and must therefore be already contained in the light.

We can see Goethe, through his whole artistic disposition, taking his place between the light and the darkness, and perceiving the colours arising through a struggle between them.

We can imagine Steiner standing consciously within the light which is itself invisible to the senses, gazing out into nature which would be all in darkness without that light, and beholding the colours arising where sensible nature reaches into the supersensible light.

Newton as observer stands within the sensible world. That is all he is concerned with and he translates the phenomena accordingly.

Goethe the artist experiences life and nature as a process of interplay between the sensible and the supersensible. He even coined the expression sensory-moral (*sinnlich-sittlich*) to describe beholding the world both with the outer senses and with inner perception of the *idea* creative in the phenomenon.

Steiner is at home in the supersensible world, and beholds the physical world in its spiritual aspect. Thus in pursuing his study of living organisms he wrote: 'I came upon the *sensible-supersensible* form of which Goethe speaks, which is interposed, both for natural vision and also for spiritual vision, between what the senses grasp and what the spirit perceives.'

This interposing realm he described later as one of etheric formative forces, which shape all forms into outer visibility. Goethe had trained himself to perceive this hidden creative ideal element at work in nature, so that he could claim actually *to see ideas* with the same clarity as others who see only outer objects. This led him to speak of the *archetypal plant* which manifests throughout the plant kingdom in varying degrees from the simplest to the highest forms. For Goethe the archetypal plant became a major discovery following many years of close study of the plant kingdom. It was there for his inner eye as a potent reality. To others, even to Schiller, it appeared to be only an abstract idea.

For Rudolf Steiner Goethe was the major discovery of his student days. And then, on the recommendation of his teacher, Karl Julius Schröer, a noted Goetheanist, it came about in 1884, when he was 23, that he was invited to edit Goethe's scientific writings 'with introductions and running explanatory commentaries', for what was to be a standard publication, Kürschner's *German National Literature* series. In order to try and make Goethe's work more understandable to others he wrote *The Theory of Knowledge Implicit in Goethe's World Conception*, published in 1886.

In 1895, he wrote a further volume, *Goethe's World Conception*. The work he undertook stretched to five volumes and was not completed until 1897. He was also invited to edit some hitherto unpublished work by Goethe lying in the archives at Weimar. He thus spent years living in Weimar with others likewise engaged in working on Goethe. That Goethe has been acknowledged as a pioneer of a new science of morphology is in large measure due to Steiner's work.

Steiner writes:

Long before Kepler and Copernicus, human beings saw the processes in the starry heavens. These two first discovered the laws underlying these occurrences. Long before Goethe, organic nature was investigated. Goethe discovered its laws. Goethe is the Copernicus and Kepler of the organic world.

Elsewhere he speaks of him similarly as the Galileo of organic nature.

Steiner also wrote a book, *Goethe as the Founder of a New Science of Aesthetics*, in which artist and scientist meet in their different yet complementary roles, a view that is close to the heart of anthroposophy.

In his work on Goethe Steiner entered deeply into Goethe's nature, seeing and interpreting the world through his eyes. Rudolf Steiner acknowledges that to carry this through, whilst continuing with his own research, required great discipline and helped him develop even greater objectivity in regard to his own work.

During these years *The Philosophy of Freedom* was shaping in his mind. This was to provide a sure foundation for the anthroposophy to come.

## *The nature of thinking* *(with reference to* The Philosophy of Freedom*)*

As the years went by, Rudolf Steiner came into close contact with many interesting people wrestling in their different ways with the problems of life. Try as he would he could find no way of communicating to them what to him was most vital. He remained isolated in himself. His endeavours to elucidate what Goethe had been striving for brought only a dubious response.

I had a conversation with a physicist who was an important person in his field and who had also devoted himself intensively to Goethe's conception of nature. The conversation came to a climax in his saying that Goethe's conception of colours was such that physics could not do anything whatever with it—and in my *becoming silent*.

How much there was then which indicated that what was truth to me was of such a character that contemporary thought 'could do nothing whatever with it'.

And so it was in all things. He was the conscious bearer of an inner world of reality of which humanity had dire need, but he could find no entry to the minds of even his closest friends. They could only conclude that capable as he was, and practical, he was nevertheless caught up in some kind of dream.

He writes:

I entered with vital intensity into what others perceived and thought, but I could not make my own inner spirituality flow into this world I thus experienced. As to my own being, I had always to remain behind within myself. Indeed, my world was separated as if by a thin veil from all the outer world . . .

Thus it was both with people, and also with philosophical approaches. I liked to be with Suphan; I liked to be with Hartleben. Suphan never called on Hartleben; Hartleben never called on Suphan. Neither could enter into the characteristic ways of thinking and feeling of the other. With Suphan and equally with Hartleben I was immediately at home. But neither Suphan nor Hartleben ever came to me. Even when they came to me, they really remained with themselves. In my spiritual world I could receive no visitor.

The question for Steiner remained: 'How can a way be found to express what I inwardly behold as true in a way that can be understood by this age?'

What is this age? It is an age when human beings set out to explore the world anew, independent of the past; an age of knowledge built on the evidence of the physical senses alone; an age of science that excludes all consideration of anything transcending the purely physical; an age therefore of scepticism and agnosticism in which only materialistic thinking prevails. From the perspective of this thinking, the human being is no more than a complex piece of matter subject to physical and chemical analysis like any other piece of matter, all his attributes being regarded as effects of matter. This is an age, therefore, in which the human being appears to have lost sight of himself.

The consequence is that the expectations of growing freedom through emancipation from past restraints has resulted in conditions of rapidly increasing unfreedom. This was becoming apparent in the nineteenth century and has become sharply evident since. Knowledge in its present form has divorced life on earth from purposeful meaning. How could someone endowed with spiritual perception speak to people in our time? This was the formidable question for Rudolf Steiner.

Many, on first coming to anthroposophy, wonder why such emphasis is placed on thinking. Rudolf Steiner states that he could have presented what he had to say in mythological form. Appealing thus through pictures and images directly to the feelings, progress might have been rapid. We live, however, in an age where the intellectual faculty is paramount, an age which prides itself on advancing its knowledge through independent observation and thought. This was therefore the rock on which he had to build.

> The form of expression in the realm of the natural sciences consists in content-filled ideas, even though the content might be materialistically conceived. I desired to form ideas that bear upon the spiritual world in the same way as scientific ideas bear upon the physical.

But how is one to regard thinking itself? Are thoughts merely the result of the impress of sense-impressions upon the mind, or are they engendered from within us to take hold of the life of the senses? In regard to this question Rudolf Steiner writes explicitly:

> In sense-perception we face the world as illusion. But when, from within ourselves, sense-free thinking engages with sense-perception, illusion is permeated with reality; it

ceases to be illusion. The human spirit experiencing itself within, then meets the Spirit of the World, now no longer concealed from us behind the sense world, but living and moving within the sense world.

So how is one to regard materialism?

I perceived the harmful character of this way of thinking not in the fact that the materialist directs his attention to the material phenomenon, but in the way he conceives matter. He contemplates *matter* without becoming aware that he is really in the presence of *spirit*, which is simply manifesting itself in the form of matter ... Spirit must first take on the form of a material brain in order, in this form, to enable the conceptual world to live and act, bestowing upon us in our earthly life freely acting self-awareness. To be sure, in the brain spirit mounts upwards out of matter, but only after the material brain has arisen out of spirit.

Rudolf Steiner is at pains to show in his later work how in the course of the ages the human spirit descended more and more deeply into matter. We will return to this later. This led, on the one hand, to a diminishing awareness of the spiritual world and, at the same time, to an accentuated awareness of self. In the present age of science this dual process has reached a climax. We find ourselves completely cut off from the spiritual world but strongly centred in our isolated sense of selfhood.

We are cut off to such an extent that we cannot even truly find our fellow human beings. Yet in this very fact lives the secret of the age, our growing need to cross the boundaries that separate us from others and from the world. What might appear superficially as the greatest loss could be the opportunity for the greatest gain. If the separation is to be surmounted by conscious effort and in freedom, it can only be, to begin with, on the basis of pure, sense-free, self-reliant thinking. Developing this could lead the science of nature to a science of the spirit, from the world of the 'seen' to the world of the 'not seen', so that we may, once again, feel ourselves united with higher reality.

At the age of 27 or 28, while deeply engaged in his work on Goethe, Rudolf Steiner was at the same time profoundly concerned with establishing a bridge from science, despite its present materialistic character, to the worlds of the spirit which were, we might say, awaiting man's call. He described the situation as he then saw it in the following way:

> Whoever recognizes as an attribute of thinking its capacity of perception extending beyond apprehension through the senses must necessarily also allow that thinking engages with objects existing beyond the limits of mere sense-perceptible realities. But these objects of thinking are ideas.
>
> As thinking takes possession of the idea, it merges with the primordial foundation of the world; external agents and realities enter into the human spirit; we become one with objective reality at its highest potency.

In other words, we are no longer confined to external perception of the world but begin to perceive, to begin with in ideas, the shaping powers at work within phenomena. (We can here recall Goethe's perception of the archetypal plant.)

Rudolf Steiner:

> I wished to express the truth that nature is in reality spiritual. I wished to show that the human being, *in thinking*, does not form conceptions about nature while standing outside her, but that knowing means *experiencing*,

so that, while knowing, we are inside the innate essence of things.

Further:

Being aware of the idea within reality is human communion.

Each has to reach and take hold of the idea himself, yet it is in this very realm that we can truly find one another in total freedom and in perfect fellowship. This is to find one another in the spirit, the first, essential step towards rediscovering the worlds of spirit.

'Thinking,' wrote Rudolf Steiner, 'has the same significance in relation to ideas as the eye has for light, the ear for sound: it is the organ of perception.'

All this is so remote from the common view of things that initially it may call for great effort to make it real to oneself, but it then comes as an amazing discovery. It means no less than that in coming to a new realization of the character of one's own thinking, we also come to a new relationship with our very selves, with our fellow human beings and with the whole world order. We begin to face life from a totally new vantage point. We are no longer wanderers astray in a strange and remote world but have a secure ground under us from which to re-examine and re-evaluate all previous values and experiences. It is thus far that Rudolf Steiner can bring us in his *Philosophy of Freedom*, published in 1894 when he was 33.

But the book was not understood. The moment it was off the press he sent a copy to the one person he thought might understand, an older man whom he revered as an enlightened thinker. He waited expectantly and full of hope. The volume came back, most painstakingly annotated with comments and observations but showing that what the book really stood for had been totally misunderstood.

However, as with the work on Goethe, so the work on *The Philosophy of Freedom* had been faithfully carried through. In the alchemy of life, and in the course of years, understanding began to grow until there are many who would say it marked a turning point in their approach to life. The book is there to be read. While it is not my intention greatly to enlarge on it here, there are some comments concerning the book which I think may be helpful.

First, there is a question. *The Philosophy of Freedom* first appeared in 1894—a long time ago. Yet it is only very rarely referred to in any academic course on philosophy. Why is that?

The answer, of course, lies in the nature of the book. It is not a philosophy as ordinarily understood, that is, as the expression of a particular thinker setting out his views on life. There are many philosophers and each one presents his personal outlook. *The Philosophy of Freedom* cannot be described in that way. It is not a Steiner philosophy, but rather a study of the nature of thinking.

Its basic principle is that thinking as an activity arises within the human being in the form of ideas or concepts. Thinking has to be about something and that something stands before one as an object perceived, a percept. Only when the concept and the percept properly meet and relate do we touch a full experience of reality. Only the human being can bring about this meeting of concept and percept—only each one for himself—in this lies the road to freedom.

*The Philosophy of Freedom* shows three levels at which this meeting takes place.

The first relates to the life of the senses. The senses bring to us a perceived object or percept. To grasp that percept in an act of cognition, we have to give birth to the answering concept. However, since every percept that comes towards us by way of the physical senses is born of the past, it follows that our conceptual life, our concepts, are likewise related to the past. This characterizes our present-day scientific outlook built as it is entirely on the 'supposed' view of the past.

The second level of meeting of concept with percept rests within the human being himself. He engenders an idea—and can contemplate this in the same way as any other percept. If we wish to have knowledge of what is thus engendered, though not of the senses, we have all the same to bring a concept towards it. It is thus that a system of mathematics arises, wholly in the mind, how Euclidean geometry was developed and more recently synthetic geometry—how a philosophy, or other construction wholly of the mind, is evolved. This is a process which rests entirely in the present. Here we are in the realm of cognitive experience, independent of the outer world of the senses, a thinking activity as a creative process which rests upon the faculty of perception which we grasp through the concept and in the immediate present.

There is a third level at which concept and percept meet. It will be seen that every thought arises as an act of intuition—it is brought to light from within. There arise in this way what Rudolf Steiner calls moral intuitions, which rise to consciousness as moral imaginations such as truth, beauty, goodness. These, too, are ideas arising in the mind, we might also say in the spirit, as percepts to be observed and met by answering concepts. Here, however, the percept by its very nature transcends our present state of being. We may have knowledge of truth, beauty, goodness but at the same time realize how far we fall short. They stand before us as a call from the 'as yet not' to the 'yet to be'. But in striving towards that future, we ourselves are changed from what we are to what we hope to become. At this level the cognitional act takes us into the future.

Thus, in so far as thinking is related to sense-experience we commune with the past; in evolving a structure of thought within ourselves we commune with the present; in the contemplation of ideas that stand before us as ideals we commune with the future.

Thinking, therefore, has a threefold character related to past, present and future. To grasp this is to meet reality in all its aspects, but the achievement can only be by individual effort as an act of freedom—hence the title of the book, *The Philosophy of Freedom*. This is just one illustration of a far-reaching exercise contained in the book. We begin to understand how with the idea we live within creation, at one with the Creator.

# 2
# ANTHROPOSOPHY, A WAY TO HIGHER KNOWLEDGE

The publication of *The Philosophy of Freedom* still left unanswered the question of how anthroposophy itself was to come into the world. To Rudolf Steiner it was clear 'that the turn of the century must bring a new spiritual light to humanity', but how was this to come about?

In 1897 he left Weimar for Berlin. Soon after his arrival there he was offered the editorship of a long established cultural magazine. After three years, seeing he could not usefully carry it further he gave it up.

At one point he was invited to speak at a private gathering of theosophists on Goethe's fairy tale. This led to a second lecture on the theme 'Goethe's secret revelation'. Of this he wrote: 'It was my basic anthroposophical lecture and the point of departure for my anthroposophical work.' There followed invitations for further lectures, even for courses of lectures which gave rise to such books as *Christianity as Mystical Fact*, *From Buddha to Christ* and *Mysticism and Modern Thought*. His audiences were still drawn mainly from the Theosophical Society with its strong leaning towards the East. He made it clear that the lectures he gave were based on his own spiritual experiences focusing on a spiritual science of the West.

He felt a strong need to found a journal of his own, hence the periodical *Lucifer-Gnosis* in 1902. 'In this periodical first appeared what I had to say about the efforts the human mind must make in order to achieve its own perception and comprehension of the spirit.' He began to present in instalment form what later comprised the book *Knowledge of Higher Worlds*.

This manner of openly communicating spiritual knowledge met with serious objections from some quarters. It was Rudolf Steiner's view, however, that the time had come when every human being had a right to whatever knowledge might be helpful to him, a view he always maintained. The opening sentence reads: 'There slumber in every human being faculties by means of which he can acquire for himself a knowledge of higher worlds.'

For ten years, from 1902 to 1912, Rudolf Steiner served as General Secretary of the German section of the Theosophical Society, though at all times pursuing his own way. Differences arose which came to a head with the announcement that a certain young Hindu was a reincarnation of Christ. The young man himself, Krishnamurti, repudiated this to his lasting credit. Such a suggestion was so utterly out of accord with the truth Rudolf Steiner knew that it marked the end of his association with that Society. Those who held with him formed the core of what then became the Anthroposophical Society.

Rudolf Steiner gave lectures to a variety of different audiences. The magazine *Lucifer-Gnosis,* however, was addressed to all. He saw it as his task to share his spiritual knowledge as widely as possible. *The Philosophy of Freedom* had paved the way for this. In his journal he set out a carefully ordered series of exercises, intimate in style as from a teacher to his pupils, yet in every sense free. They are intended to lead by sure and certain stages along a path of inner development. The initiative, however, is left for each one to take according to his own independent judgement.

## Types of exercises

No more will be attempted here than to indicate in an elementary way the nature and scope of some of the initial exercises and how they relate to one another.

For anyone embarking seriously on a path to higher knowledge there are certain prerequisites to be observed. They seem obvious yet need to be mentioned. First and foremost, Rudolf Steiner stresses the need to cultivate reverence for life and devotion to truth; then to strive always for clear thinking, balanced feeling, and a steadfast will; further, to continually keep in mind the *golden rule*: For every step in knowledge, three steps in moral development. The goal of one's striving is service to life. It is good to recognize how far we have all been the victims, from birth on, of the negative effects of mass media and mechanization. The exercises, in addition to all else, are restorative of health; they aim to make us whole. We stand in certain relationships to life simply through our constitution as human beings: our relationship to the world around us through our physical senses; our relationship to time through the force of memory without which we should be utterly lost; then our dependence on others in the course of the years, from birth onwards, in the shaping of our biography; finally, what we owe to ourselves in motivating our own endeavours. The four exercises we are about to describe follow, in the main, the opening sections of *Knowledge of Higher Worlds*.

The first relates to the life of the senses. We place a plant before us and observe it with all the care possible. We regard its form, colour, the succession of its parts, and so on. We then reflect on what we cannot see, the living entity that maintains and shapes the plant from stage to stage. The plant, as regards our senses, is part 'seen', part 'not seen', part revealed and part concealed. The part 'not seen' is waiting for us to develop another, a higher form of seeing. We repeat this exercise day after day, uniting our reflections with the accompanying feelings. This develops a gentle quality of alertness for all that meets us in life, part revealed and part concealed. As with all such exercises, our responsibility rests on the faithfulness with which we carry them out. Having performed the exercise we set it aside and proceed with our normal day's work. We do not live in anticipation of results but rest upon the doing. The fruits will show themselves in their own time.

The next exercise calls for a similar heightening of attentiveness, this time towards the sphere of memory. In the course of a day we pass through a host of impressions. It is as though life were beckoning to us at every turn. What we have consciously observed we can recall as pictures in the mind.

This is quite a different seeing from that of the senses. We are gazing into a realm concealed from the outer senses, that of time. Let us select one of the many situations in which we find ourselves and recreate it as vividly as possible. But now we must be careful not to look back merely introspectively, focusing our attention on ourselves in order to re-experience subjectively what we have already experienced. The aim of the exercise is, rather, that we look away from ourselves to all that surrounded us at the time. If we were enjoying a sunset then we focus on the sunset itself that called forth the joy in us. Was it a child in his innocent play that drew our attention, or a beggar by the wayside? Was it a stranger who came knocking on our door to ask the way? Was it a familiar or an unfamiliar voice on the telephone bringing good news, bad news? Was it the sight of the early snowdrops lifting their heads from the ground? What a host of eventfulness surrounds us all the time, playing towards us, with us, in us! Whatever it was that was outside us is now within us, it has entered into the stream of time, *our* time. Outside in space it might have been for all to see and experience. Now it has become an intrinsic part of ourselves, present for us alone. Memory gives us a ground to stand on, a ground of con-

tinuity within the otherwise vanishing passage of time. Time
is no longer a juxtaposition of events occurring in space. The
world of time reveals itself as an unfolding into space. We see
it unfolding in the plant. We see it unfolding in the child, in
ourselves also—a manifestation of growing and becoming
and passing away. It is really time that carries space in its
arms.

The physical body that I see with my eyes is perpetually
changing, being cast off and recreated, it is said, every seven
years. Physical substance is in a constant state of flow but the
image and form is retained. So, too, events pass by, but the
memory remains. External form and memory belong
together. They are manifestations of what we may call a time-
body or, in anthroposophy, an etheric or formative force
body. It is the world out of which the visible world is shaped
and we ourselves participate in that world, are as it were
membered in it. To us is given the power to re-member ourselves in thought into situations that have passed.

As the first exercise belongs to the world of the senses, the
senses being part of our physical body, so we have a body in
the realm of time. We are consciously living in a process of
time and our awareness of ourselves is built on our memories.
With the first exercise relating to the plant we also become
aware of a time process, but one outside us. With the second
exercise we are ourselves within the time process.

The third exercise also relates to time but differently. We
are concerned now with events and encounters which break in
on the course of our lives, bringing major changes in the
tenor, the direction, even the character of our lives. We meet a
stranger who becomes a close associate, maybe even an intimate friend, a partner in life, perhaps through marriage or in
some other connection. We live through an illness or maybe a
serious accident which marks a turning point in our life. We

experience the death of someone close to us and confront the mystery of death as never before; this may well lead to a deepening of our whole attitude to life. We pick up a book, as though by chance, and it may be the starting point of a new quest in life. We waken with an idea which opens up a new vista for us, and so on. What may not happen in the course of a lifetime? Are such events, which come like interventions, to be attributed only to chance? In retrospect they play a most significant part in shaping our lives and in determining our biography. We select one or another such experience in our life, something preferably that happened some time ago so that we are not immediately emotionally involved. Again and again as we confront such a past experience, recalling the people who have entered our life at this or that point in our history, the impression may grow in us that there is indeed another world beyond those of space and time, a world to which we owe the drama of existence with its pains and joys, its meetings and partings, now comedy and now tragedy, laughter and tears, a world that pervades all life. To this world also belongs the Mystery of the Fall and the hope of redemption—and the dream that this old, old world will one day grow young again.

But now, to return to the exercise in question, to perform it truly requires the greatest possible degree of objectivity, of freedom from self. Here more than ever one must be careful not to fall into introspection, but to learn to regard oneself with the calmness of a judge confronting a stranger. This way of looking at things opens new possibilities. We may have suffered a bereavement. Our neighbour has suffered a similar loss. Ordinarily our grief at our own loss far outweighs the sorrow we share with our neighbour. Yet it must be possible to ascend to a height, beyond things personal, from which we can contemplate the two events side by side with Godlike calmness—a level of experience where the words ring true, 'love thy neighbour as thyself', or even 'love thine enemy'. This is a level to which this exercise points, though it may seem far beyond our present capacity to achieve.

Yet the fruits of the first two exercises are with us. We are less fettered to our personality than we were before. When we have laid aside our personality in death, will we not be entering a world where quite other rules hold sway? And what does it mean in spiritual life to die to oneself? Such an exercise, if faithfully pursued, cleanses one of excess self-love and egotism. We are membered in a third world through that in us which is the bearer of impulses, desires, passions, hopes and frustrations, that part in us which does, indeed, carry the dramatic struggle of our inner life. In addition to a physical body and an etheric body, anthroposophy speaks of an astral body related to the world of the stars (aster—a star), in which, for example, the ancient Egyptians and other peoples could read factors influencing earthly human destiny. Through this third exercise we may learn to attain positive acceptance of our destiny whatever it may bring, and contemplate our trials with a measure of equanimity and even thankfulness.

Beyond the physical body, beyond the life or etheric body, beyond the desire or astral body, is the human ego of which these are the sheaths. The fourth exercise in this series relates to the human ego. The three bodies give shape and expression to the outer personality. The ego is the core of our being; it is at one and the same time our innermost being and that in us which is universally human. Only an ego can know itself as distinct from all that surrounds it and establish conscious relationship with all. Only an ego can think. The fourth exercise has to do with thinking. It introduces us to the nature of meditation.

We select a thought that extends beyond the personal and applies equally to all human beings, a thought that is born out of deep experience and carries the testimony of its own truth within it.

Such a thought might be: 'The heights of the spirit can only be climbed by passing first through the portals of humility.' We place such a thought in the centre of our consciousness and try repeatedly to immerse ourselves in it to the exclusion of all else. We do not think about it in an abstract sense. In the stillness of our soul we strive to live it. For most of us this requires a great effort of will but the earlier exercises have already partly prepared us. There can come a time when the thought itself becomes a portal of entry to communion in thought, to communion in spirit with a world of beings. To quote Rudolf Steiner:

> Thus he now shifts the central point of his being to the inner part of his nature. He listens to the voices within him, which speak to him, in his moments of tranquillity; he cultivates exchange and dialogue with the spiritual world . . . He discovers that something living expresses itself in his thought world. He sees that his thoughts do not merely harbour shadow-pictures but that through them hidden beings speak to him. Formerly sound reached him only through his ear; now it resounds through his soul. An inner language, an inner world is revealed to him.

The four exercises have been so described as to give a first impression of the nature of anthroposophical inner work. As exercises, it will be seen, they are transparently clear. Yet because they are born of initiation knowledge, the order in which they occur is significant—thus, from the point of view from which they are given, they comprise a whole human entity. At the same time they provide a starting point for great truths still to be discovered. Through our four members, body, life, soul and spirit, we are related to four kingdoms of nature, the mineral, plant and animal and, in its own distinct character, the human kingdom.

But we are also related to kingdoms above us. Nature, the divine in nature, has brought us to our present state of being. It now rests with us, in freedom, to carry our evolution further. What we have presented so far is contained in the first part of *Knowledge of Higher Worlds*. That part ends with the following words:

> Spiritual science gives the means of developing the spiritual eyes and ears, and kindling the spiritual light; the method of spiritual training may be described as consisting of three stages. *Probation*: this develops the spiritual senses. *Enlightenment*: this kindles the spiritual light. *Initiation*: this establishes intercourse with higher spiritual beings.

## Stages of initiation

These three stages have always existed in the mystery schools of the past though the conditions will have been different. The demands on the student deepen and increase as the work advances from stage to stage.

For instance, the exercise described for the observation of the plant can carry us a long way. But now, at a later stage, comes a further exercise: to bring our attention to bear on the plant budding and blossoming, and then again, the plant wilting and withering. To help us, Rudolf Steiner compares the experience of budding and blossoming to that of a sunrise, the wilting and withering not as one might expect to a sunset but to the rising of the moon. A sunrise—a moonrise. Here is an instance to show that in spiritual matters one cannot rely on simple logic—the realities may call for quite different images. This exercise would lead to a heightened experience of all that is coming into being and passing away in nature— eventually to an awakening to the etheric world.

The following is an exercise which requires an even greater degree of concentration. The student has before him a seed, and alongside this the mere likeness of a seed. While contemplating the seed, he may call up in imagination all the possible development that is there. Turning to the non-seed, he may experience intensely how by no stretch of imagination can anything be expected to arise or unfold there. It is important to have the objects before one—not merely think them in the abstract.

So we could pass on to an exercise contrasting the experience of a crystal in its form and expression to that of an animal driven hither and thither by desire and instinct, and then direct attention to a plant as holding an intermediary position between mineral and animal.

There are exercises to do with listening which bring quite other faculties to bear: listening to a bell, for example, then to the cries and calls of an animal and then to the speech of a human being.

All these exercises call for clear thinking and strengthened feeling, for patient repetition, for the right quality of devotion, and the right degree of concentration.

The *seeing* exercises lead more towards Imagination, the *listening* exercises towards Inspiration. Intuition requires before all else the cultivation of love for the world and for all beings.

To make more clear what is meant by the greater freedom of human beings today, we might look briefly at an earlier time. Rudolf Steiner has described some of the mystery centres of the past.

It is hard to imagine how strictly guarded these mystery schools were from the public. To divulge any of their teachings merited death. Aeschylus was once in this danger but was able to prove his innocence. We will imagine we are in ancient Egypt. Someone approaches the temple gates. He wishes to enter as a pupil, a neophyte. He is met by a sage from within the temple, a hierophant or initiate. After a searching interview, instead of being admitted right away he may be advised to remain longer in the world outside, to exercise his natural gifts and qualities further, maybe to work for a time with the sick or the needy in some poor area, to explore what other unused capacities he might have; in any case to cultivate a regular devotional life, to establish an inner state of balance in thought and word and deed, especially in dealing with others, and then to come back. All this would have corresponded to what we have indicated as preliminary conditions.

Once entered, a life of discipline awaits him under strict guidance. He is first admitted to the outer court only, where he is led through stringent tests and trials to cultivate higher vision—this would correspond to what we have called probation leading through a process of purification to conscious spiritual Imagination. Then, when he is considered sufficiently prepared, the ruling powers of the temple decide to admit him to the middle court, where even severer disciplines await him; where he may have to live through extremes of fear beyond anything normally known, and great enticements of soul (we may think of the temptations that Buddha underwent on the eve of enlightenment, or the trials and temptations of St Anthony). This eventually leads to actual communion with divine beings, which we might call conscious spiritual Inspiration. A long and even more arduous path awaits him before he can hope to merit entry into the innermost court, the holy of holies; there he would have to experience the laying aside of his personality, eliminating the last trace of self-love, to all intents and purposes dying to himself in a death-sleep of three-day duration—always under the immensely watchful and unremitting care of his initiate teachers. Such would be the path towards conscious spiritual Intuition—a state of oneness with the divine. He might then be called on to go back as a master into life, as a guide and teacher to his fellow human beings.

This brief sketch may show how our inner life conforms to eternal divine laws. Today the onus rests on each one to determine his own way. Anthroposophy opens a way which each may follow.

Even at the most elementary stage Rudolf Steiner is able to bring what concerns the very highest in us into forms which can be grasped, understood and practised in daily life. There is no question at any point of blind dependence, of placing one's will under the jurisdiction of another. These higher truths live germinally in all. From this point of view, let us glance once again at the terms Imagination—living in images; Inspiration—living through the Word; Intuition—discovering and uniting with divine being.

We meet someone for the first time. To begin with we have only an outer impression of the person, an image. The moment real conversation begins between us, things become very different. We reveal something of our being, the one to the other. The world comes to life between us. There is no longer mere image. If our communication is a true one, we inspire one another with new-found riches. We become friends. This friendship may grow and deepen until a genuine love grows up between us. We begin to know one another from within. That is also Intuition, the capacity to enter into one another—this intuitive knowing from within is to love. Thus we see how these gifts that we bring towards one another are at the same time the incipient beginnings of what may grow and unfold into the three stages of higher consciousness: beholding, communing, divining. The seed forces for such a higher development are present in all of us.

Anthroposophy speaks of:

*Conscious Imagination:* beholding the world as image of the divine in its working and weaving.

*Conscious Inspiration:* communing with the divine, revelation of the Word in nature.

*Conscious Intuition:* growing to be one with the divine—in older language, becoming one with God.

These are the three stages implied by the words Probation, Enlightenment, Initiation.

We use the terms imagination, inspiration, intuition in referring to artists, poets, creative thinkers. We regard them quite truly as gifts welling up from unconscious depths, carrying experience beyond the mundane and commonplace. Before a great work of art we feel 'translated' as though raised to another level of being.

In anthroposophy these terms are employed to mean an actual awakening in full consciousness to those realms from which these experiences reach us, an awakening to the beings in higher worlds connected with human destiny and waiting for human beings to awaken to them for the greater well-being of the world as a whole; they have not relinquished us, though we in our materialistic age appear to have forgotten them.

## *The basic books*

Anthroposophy offers various approaches to the question of inner development but they all meet in the one end goal, our awakening to our own true being and thereby also to the spiritual foundation of all existence.

What we have presented so far relates particularly to the first part of *Knowledge of Higher Worlds*, the part that was originally entitled *The Way of Initiation*. The second half, *Initiation and its Results*, seemingly offers a different approach but actually supplements and illuminates the first part. It is not a case of choosing the one way or the other. The student is entirely free to choose from each or both what appears to him to suit him best. The second part, like the first, follows a given order. It offers exercises for the shaping and perfecting of certain soul and spirit organs of perception even as nature has provided clearly shaped sense organs for knowing the physical world. It goes on to describe resulting changes of consciousness first in dream life and then in waking life. We are led to the first full encounter with oneself in what is described as the meeting with the Guardian of the Threshold, and thence, eventually, to a meeting with the Greater Guardian at the threshold of death. We think of Odysseus crossing the River Styx to the realm of Hades to bring back from the dead new powers for the guidance of the living. Here again is an example of how Rudolf Steiner quite typically unfolds from the very beginning a view that carries through to the end so that, though we confront mysteries to be resolved, we never need feel left in the dark.

The book *Theosophy* is also an early work, published in 1904. (The title of the book has no connection with the Theosophical Society.) The book describes someone walking across a meadow. He discovers a threefold relationship between himself and the world around him. First he views himself from outside simply as a body amongst bodies. Next he recalls his memories of that same meadow a year ago, compares his experiences then and now, and thus recognizes an inner life which belongs to him alone, and which, to begin with, may be called soul. But then, a student of botany, he explores and discovers the laws and conditions of plant life. The truths he discovers are equally true for all people. To this capacity to transcend the personal and achieve the universal may be assigned the name spirit. The recognition that man is a being of body, soul and spirit provides the ground plan for the whole book. This threefold nature is elaborated further into a sevenfold and even a ninefold human being within the total evolutionary process. The description carries us beyond death to the experiences the soul passes through in the soul world, the spirit in the spirit world. The laws of metamorphosis translate the past into a new future, in other words, are resolved into the laws of reincarnation. The human being finds himself once more upon the earth. All he has lived through in body, soul and spirit is gathered up into a re-encounter with the circumstances of a new earthly existence. The book ends with still another approach to initiation.

*Occult Science, an Outline*, 1908, is likewise a basic book. The use of the word 'occult' in the title belies its original meaning for what was once held hidden has here been made 'an open secret'. The book recapitulates, again somewhat differently, the main contents of *Knowledge of Higher Worlds* and *Theosophy*. Its main contribution, however, lies in the comprehensive survey it gives of world and human evolution. To this we will return later.

Over the years other approaches became possible, illuminated through religion, the arts, the humanities, the sciences and practical social life, all converging, however, in the one great central task: the redemption of the image of man from its present fallen state and the awakening to his true being as central to the whole evolutionary process.

# 3

# ASPECTS OF THE HUMAN BEING

## *Man and nature*

Anthroposophy is concerned primarily with understanding the human being. An immediate question is that of our relationship to the kingdoms around us, mineral, plant and animal. Darwin could foresee no bridge being built from mineral to plant, that is, from the non-living to the living, or from plant to animal. He conceived the idea that human and ape must have had a common ancestor and that, therefore, there was no such sharp dividing line between animal and man—hence his *Origin of Species* and *Descent of Man.* So far the supposed 'missing link' between ape and human being has evaded all search. Despite fossil finds since Darwin's day, no creature living or in the fossil past has been declared as our actual ancestor.

Teilhard de Chardin goes to great lengths in his *Phenomenon of Man* to show that *thinking* could not have been derived either from animal instinct or even from animal intelligence at its highest level. He concludes that the birth of thought in the human being can only be regarded as a special act of creation. Goethe saw the human being with his upright carriage and conscious life of striving as standing at the peak of nature so that in him nature itself is raised further into art, science, religion and human culture generally. Goethe's immersion in the living processes of nature enabled him to say, when confronting a Greek work of art: 'This is necessity, this is God.'

Today's dominant concept of physical continuity from the

most elementary particle to the most highly evolved organism leaves no entry for the human spirit. The human being is still regarded as an animal, a highly advanced animal, even a thinking animal, but still an animal: animal cries are the precursors of the human word, animal instincts the fore-runners of human conduct and morality. In the world of orthodox science no higher concept of the human being has yet been admitted.

Anthroposophy takes a different approach. It reviews four basic phenomena which we can all recognize: form, life, sentience (a consciousness based on sense-experience) and selfhood (an awareness of the self). It is these four primary phenomena we will need to consider, for all four remain unfathomable mysteries (whatever theories may be pro-pounded) in modern fields of knowledge. As our point of departure we may say: *form* we share with mineral, plant, and animal; *life* we share with plant and animal; *sensory experi-ence* we share with the animal (instincts, desires, joy and pain, etc.). *Thinking*, that is, a reflective consciousness, an inborn sense of self or the I AM is something that we human beings alone, in the world of nature, possess.

In exploring new ways into the future, anthroposophy also pays high regard to what lived as ruling wisdom in the past and has since been forgotten. It therefore turns its attention to the four classical elements which played such a big role in earlier times right back to ancient India as we will endeavour to show later, but here we will turn specially to ancient Greece. (A feeling for the four elements lived on through the Middle Ages.) We refer to the four elements, earth, water, air and fire.

Once, during a formal inspection of Michael Hall School in Forest Row (the first English-speaking Rudolf Steiner school) the science inspector came across these terms in a child's notebook. He wanted to know how such 'Aristotelian terms' had found their way into a science notebook. The teacher tried to explain that in his understanding these terms were not to be taken in their merely physical meaning. He regarded them, rather, as relating to dynamic powers working through the whole of nature; that is how he understood them to have been regarded in Greek times, not only by Aristotle. The kind of thinking which could grasp the mineral kingdom was not adequate for the plant kingdom, nor were thoughts about the plant kingdom adequate for the animal kingdom, nor could thoughts related to animals be adequate for understanding the human being. These four dynamics in nature called for discriminating qualities in human thinking and it was to demonstrate this that the teacher had introduced these classical terms. They were the best he could find. The inspector, after a silent pause, said he thought he understood, though he would probably not have used the word 'dynamics'. This is quoted here to show that to an open mind the approach, one might even say, the rediscovery of these four elements, can be full of suggestive meaning. That inspector was an exceptionally open-minded person on other counts as well.

But to return now to our main exposition. With the term 'earth' can be associated the individualizing power that manifests in all the multitudinous, distinctly recognizable forms in the mineral, plant and animal kingdoms, and also in the human kingdom where every individual person carries his own distinct identity.

Every *form* as we perceive it has been engendered in the first place out of 'water' or the fluid element which itself, at most, has only the form of a drop. The globe of the earth is such a drop in which there float the mineral masses.

Crystals come into form and even grow in a medium of

water. However, when 'water' in its dynamic character penetrates 'earth' as it does in the plant, then we arrive at forms endowed with life. There is an unfolding of form from within outwards. We may say that in the plant the water has become an inner principle—it has become the bearer of life. Whatever is living owes its life to the active presence of water. The human being is far more 'water' than he is 'earth'.

In the plant, then, we see earth penetrated by water, form combined with life.

The plants live in a medium of surrounding air and warmth.

When air penetrates living nature as an inner principle, the rhythmic process of respiration arises and with it the birth of sensory nature—animal nature is born. The more penetrating the airy process, the more highly are the senses developed, and with them the nervous system. We need only compare, let us say, a fish with a bird. Nerve, circulation, metabolism, take their measure from the breath. In the invertebrate the balance of these has a different character but it is still the penetration of the element air that is decisive. *Anima* can be translated as breath.

In the animal then, we have the three elements earth, water, air, giving rise to form imbued with life, and endowed with sensory experience or soul. The surrounding medium not yet incorporated fully is the element of 'warmth' (fire).

When warmth penetrates the three elements of earth, water and air as an inner principle, then, at the highest level of animal life the warm-blooded creatures arise, the birds, mammals and also the human being. By warm-blooded is meant the creature's capacity to engender warmth as required and to regulate it to meet varying conditions, winter and summer. This the bird can do, but the reptile cannot—hence the reptile and creatures below it are called cold-blooded.

Reptiles go into a coma with cold and into a torpor with heat, in both cases suffering a subduing of consciousness. This internalizing of warmth capacities is accompanied by social features: the care of the young, bird calls, animal calls.

But now, in the human being, this inner warmth takes on a totally new dimension, that of conscious love, a life in ideals to the point of sacrifice, devotion to the highest, new creations beyond the bounds of nature. The element of 'fire' in nature transmutes in the human being into spiritual fire, and creative endeavour.

We see the human being surrounded by the mineral, plant and animal kingdoms, yet in his innermost being standing within his own kingdom which leads him out of bondage to nature towards the realization of the divine. He gazes out at nature, responsive and responsible, yet able to say: 'My kingdom is not of this world.'

## *Thinking, feeling, will*

Human beings can look both outwards and inwards. Looking outwards we behold the world of nature and ourselves as part of that world. Looking inwards we behold ourselves in thinking, feeling and will. The world around us conforms to certain laws and conditions. Changes in the order of things can be traced to outer causes. We, too, are subject to these laws and conditions. In our life of thinking, feeling and will, however, we carry our own law within us out of which to direct our life.

Ideally a human being should be master of himself; but in fact he is only partly so. His thoughts can run away with him. His feelings can rise up unbidden. To maintain a clear line of thought is not always easy. To maintain an even command of feeling is mostly difficult. Compared with thought and feeling our will remains dark to us unless roused to action. We can be driven to act on the spur of the moment and then are left to reflect on the consequences. On the other hand an impulse can light up as a sudden thought, even as a flash of genius.

Both instincts and intuitions rise up from the hidden depths of will. They should not be confused; the former come with compulsive force, the latter as guiding messages. Sometimes the will pervades the life of feeling unaccountably with a sense of expectancy, or maybe with foreboding as though anticipatory of some future.

All this belongs to the inner drama of the life of the soul playing between the light of thought and the stirrings of will, with the life of feeling mediating between them, lending colour to a thought, or itself aglow and afire with a prompting of will. There is a Greek image of a charioteer having to keep under control three horses, all at the same time. Thinking, feeling and will are the three horses.

In the normal course of life we are awake by day, asleep by night, with dreams arising between. However, we can ask to what extent we are truly awake in the day. A little consideration will show that we are really fully awake only in our thinking. We can be so absorbed in thought as to grow oblivious to what is going on around us. As an inexperienced driver we have to keep our thoughts concentrated on every detail of what we are doing; later we may drive with a minimum of thought, simply out of habit, whilst our mind is mainly engaged elsewhere. In so simple an action as picking up a pencil to write something down, we obviously need to think about what we are doing, but, as regards the actual doing, apart from calling the will into action, in its intrinsic nature the will remains completely hidden from us. In recalling the events of a day, only what we have observed consciously in thought stands out clearly for us.

Some things we recall in a kind of haze and a great deal has passed us by completely for we were simply not awake to it. We thus confront the fact that even in our waking day we are in part awake, in part adream, and in part asleep. We are awake in our thinking, we dream in our feeling, but as regards our will, we are as asleep to it by day as we are by night. Yet these three faculties of thinking, feeling and will are for ever interacting. We could not exercise our thinking were there not some element of will present, nor could we reach down to grasp an intuition of will without the light of our thinking directed to it. Feeling is always in some measure involved.

This threefold nature of thinking, feeling and will related to waking, dreaming and sleeping is one aspect of our inner life. There is another connected with the quality of consciousness with which we apprehend life itself. We may distinguish four such qualities: intellectual, imaginative, inspirational, and intuitive.

Through the force of intellect we become immediately conscious of the world as it first meets us.

Where feeling enters into our perceptual faculty, as was the case with Goethe, we pass from external knowledge to insight; not only the thinker but also the artist in us is born. With Imagination we enter *into* the phenomena we behold. The visual arts, painting and sculpture, lead us on the way to Imagination. Feeling, however, enters into all the arts.

Music is a 'hearing' art. A musician can hear tones that reach beyond the ear. We need only think of Beethoven who never heard the greatness of his music as others do, yet who drew that music from a source. All true music sounds into the world out of what Pythagoras described as the harmony of the spheres. Here we come closer to the faculty of Inspiration.

There is a listening beyond the silence which poets also know. Poetry, the art of the word, belongs to what is innermost in us: 'In the beginning was the Word.' It carries us towards the realm of Intuition where we become one with divine being.

There is no question here of framing fixed categories but of recognizing these different qualities, each with its own significance in human life. The works of architects, sculptors, painters, also *speak* to us. There are musicians who are descriptive and imaginative. One might say that amongst English poets Keats lived more in the quality of Imagination, Shelley in that of Inspiration, and Wordsworth in Intuition, but clearly all three qualities lived in each of them and each, in his art, gave birth to profound thoughts. Anthroposophy can lead us to see how each of the four qualities of consciousness, as we have described them, has its particular seat within the total nature of the human being.

To reduce experience to thought forms in intellectual life becomes possible because the human being possesses a physical organ, the brain, as an instrument. The brain, in its perfect formation within the physical body, relates to the element 'earth'.

The faculty of Imagination rests in equal measure upon the ever flowing, ever shaping and renewing quality of 'water' in which is reflected the life body or etheric body.

Inspiration relates to the breath, to the inbreathing and outbreathing, the toning and intoning of the astral body, dependent in earthly life upon the element 'air'.

The life of Intuition is rooted in the creative fire force within us, the ego dwelling in the element of 'warmth'.

Combining this with what has gone before we can conclude the summary as follows:

| Earth | Water | Air | Fire |
|---|---|---|---|
| Physical body | Etheric body | Astral or Soul body | Ego |
| Intellectual faculty | Imaginative faculty | Inspirational faculty | Intuitive faculty |

## The threefold human organism

In 1917, after thirty years of spiritual-scientific research, as he himself tells us, Rudolf Steiner first presented his description of the threefold organism. He describes how the body consists of three distinct though closely related organizations, a nerve-sense system centred in the head, a rhythmic-circulatory system centred in the chest, and a metabolic-limb system centred in the abdomen. These three systems are co-active in every part of the body; where there is nerve there is blood, and along with the blood, respiration and metabolism. They represent three different principles: the nerve-sense system comprising brain, nerves and senses is related to the conscious life of thought; the rhythmic-circulatory system comprising lung, heart and circulation, as the centre of the body's rhythmic functioning, to the life of feeling; and the limb-metabolic system (limb and metabolism being inseparable in their functioning) to the life of will.

Through these three systems we stand in three relationships to our environment. In the head we receive sense-impressions and meet them with our answering thoughts as described earlier. In the chest we take in oxygen and give back the carbon dioxide produced by the body. In our abdomen, the seat of the digestive process, we take in the foodstuffs which we reduce to solubility, pass them through the intestinal walls by a process of absorption, and the resulting lymph is then carried into the blood for the further process of assimilation. Thus there is catabolism or the breaking down of the substances of outer nature, and anabolism, the corresponding synthesis of substances within the organism, processes which science can record but can by no means explain in physical terms alone. In the head we engage in the world process through the refined nature of our sense-perceptions, in the chest through the subtle element of air, in the abdomen through the heavier elements of water and earth, here using the term 'elements' as introduced earlier. There is thus intensification of substance process from the head down, and accentuation of consciousness process from below up. In the head, the consciousness pole, metabolism is most reduced; in the abdomen where metabolism is at its most intense, consciousness is most dimmed. In the middle system, the rhythmic-circulatory, we oscillate between enhanced consciousness on breathing in and a diminution of consciousness on breathing out. We enter earthly life on the first inbreath and leave the world again on the last outbreath.

The interplay of the three soul forces of thinking, feeling and will via the threefold bodily organism has been closely studied since it was first described in 1917. It plays greatly into the practice of education, medicine, the social sciences, and many other aspects of our relationship to the world. It is understandable that this view of the threefold organism is highly challenging to much of modern theory but, as we have already indicated, the modern outlook includes a great deal of questioning of our present state of knowledge, with the awakening of many people, not least amongst scientists, to a sense that there are new boundaries to be crossed. It is very much a question of the approach to these matters. There is no likelihood of progress so long as one persists in the view that the human being is no more than the material body perceptible to the physical senses.

At a recent conference convened by young people of 17 to

19, approaching the end of their schooling or having recently left, the following question arose, 'How are we to understand such terms as material and spiritual?' Since these two terms are loaded with ambiguities and possible misconceptions, a different approach to the question was offered by substituting for material and spiritual the terms, sensible and super-sensible. By sensible we mean everything accessible to the senses—that is quite clear. But now, turning to the human being, he lives in his thoughts, his feelings, his will. Thinking or thoughts are not accessible to the senses, yet we are fully aware of them—they are beyond sense-experience, super-sensible. Likewise feelings and the will are supersensible. Thus our inner life is supersensible. What we see of the human being with the senses belongs to the material world. What, then, of what we do not see with the senses? It is possible to develop inner faculties through inner schooling, then we can grow aware that, just as in our physical body we belong to the material world, the world of the senses, so through our supersensible nature we belong to a supersensible world of supersensible facts and beings. That is what the great teachers of humanity were able to reach. Through inner schooling, through heightening the faculties they possessed as thinking, feeling and will, they raised themselves to higher worlds. As spiritual teachers they did not theorize; they bore witness to the spirit. Once we begin to recognize that our inner life is supersensible, all that remains is to train this further. But there is one condition, that we should train the faculties we already possess in order to acquire true knowledge and understanding of the world of the senses. This is essential as preparation for a higher seeing and knowing later. The young people I mentioned felt they had been well served—they could relate to the terms sensible and supersensible in a way they could work with.

There are obstacles to be overcome when it comes to understanding the functioning of the threefold organism. One is the misconception that *all* human experience, thinking, feeling and will, is centred, controlled and directed by the head, meaning the brain. The brain as an organ is most perfectly formed and marvellously related to the organism as a whole, but in itself it is the most effete, having less recuperative power and vitality than any other organ in the body. In so far as thinking is an activity, a function of will, it cannot originate in the brain. Rudolf Steiner likens the brain to a mirror; it reflects what is otherwise life and impulse and action in the form of abstract thoughts, mirror images without substance. Only if we bring will and feeling into these shadow thoughts do they take on life, become *living* thoughts with which to take hold of reality. We see in the world today how ineffectual is abstract thinking, unable to grasp and enter into what is really calling; thus we are drowned in questions which remain unanswered and lead to frustration and violent protest. It is soul and spirit that are calling out of intuitive depths for consciousness to awaken out of the sleep of materialism.

Another immense challenge is to the idea that the heart is a pump. The real challenge lies in the lack of understanding of the true nature of blood, which continues to be regarded as a vegetative fluid. In fact it is the bearer of the warmth element, the fire in us. How this warmth or fire is generated, how maintained, how it enters the will and empowers the mind, are questions waiting to be answered. Blood is the most vital tissue in the body, so vital that it continues in a flowing state, this continually self-renewing blood through whose unceasing working all the organs and tissues of the body are constantly reinvigorated. Blood is the very antithesis of what Rudolf Steiner describes as the 'dying nerve'. Blood appears in the embryo first; then, formed by the ever-flowing blood, the heart gradually develops. The heart is created by the blood to serve the blood. Great problems to be solved by future science are involved here as in the question of the functioning of the brain.

And another basic error lives in the view that the human being is simply a continuation of the food he eats. Such a view, though not always expressed so crudely, ignores the hidden realities that underlie the three stages of digestion, absorption and assimilation. It also ignores the amazing fact of what it is, in all this flux of continuous action of breaking down and building up, that faithfully maintains the image, the uniqueness of each single individual as a member of the human race.

## *The growing child*

There is no better way of confirming the reality of the threefold human being as he develops in body, soul and spirit than by studying the growing child. Clearly the three faculties of thinking, feeling and will and their relationship to the adult have first to be evolved in the course of the years.

The child at birth is the most helplessly dependent of all creatures. The little songbird soon grows strong and spreads its wings. The mammal offspring cling to their dams a while but very soon find their legs. But what a long and complex process of gradual emancipation awaits the child!

There lies the newborn infant just as we laid him down, with his large head, too heavy to lift, and his diminutive limbs with their movements quite undirected. Within a year that child, after many trials, will have lifted himself unaided to the upright position and have begun to walk. That is the great achievement of the first year, beginning from the limbs. Then we hear the child practising language sounds, and in the course of the second year words are formed, speech has begun. In the course of the third year words are framed to express thoughts which flash up and are quickly gone.

First movements of limbs, then more delicate movements of speech, then the most refined movements of all in the awakening of thought—it is this sequence that Rudolf Steiner stressed as being most important, the awakening process from limb to chest to head.

Then comes a thought which can only arise by intuition with the utterance of the word 'I', and conscious memory finds its beginning; autobiography is born.

This sequence of the first three years of infancy finds its repetition on a greater scale in the three stages of childhood: infancy, the primary years, and adolescence. Rudolf Steiner education (also called Waldorf education) is based on observation of this sequence, with all its intermediate stages.

In the infant years the child grows into life by absorbing and imitating whatever comes to him from the environment. During these early years when body metabolism, assimilation and growing are most intensive, this imitation goes deepest, and has effects for the whole of life. Love, harmony, beauty flowing to the child translate into health, confidence, physical and moral strength, whereas indifference, discord, ugly and chaotic conditions result in discouragement, insecurity, distrust and possible aggression. It is by imitation that the child acquires refined and beautiful or coarse and ugly speech. It is in imitating mother or father in what they are doing that the child should find a natural training for capable and meaningful actions and abilities in later life. All this continues into the infant school (kindergarten and nursery), which is scarcely needed where home life is favourably adjusted to the child. Once in the nursery and kindergarten, the learning process continues by nurturing above all a limb-learning process through activity. The child in these years is not yet contemplative, does not yet stand back and *think about* but rather *beholds* and in his own way *recognizes* and *knows*; during the limb-learning stage consciousness is still predominantly intuitive in character. In the primary school years, from the beginning of the change of teeth to puberty, the child enters into a quite different sense of relationship with home, school and the surrounding world. Here, at the second stage, education rests essentially upon what the teacher can tell, upon the word. It is through the descriptive power of the word, be it in the early years through fairy tales and legends or in the later years through history and biography, and in an artistic introduction to nature, that the child chiefly learns—no longer by imitation as in the infant years but by identifying himself with the picture, growing one with the picture. The right image brought to the child nourishes the heart and strengthens feeling life. The immense damage done in these years by the false or destructive image can hardly be imagined. But also the word as human expression may be seen in a wider sense to include the arts, painting, modelling, music, poetry, drama, eurythmy (a new art of movement based on speech and tone), gymnastics, and the crafts. In the middle years it is limb and heart that are engaged quite specially; the thinking should be colourful, inspirational and imaginative, not yet cooled to the abstract. On entering the adolescent years at puberty there is a radical change, both in body and in soul, reflected in a strong awakening to the personal. Education now enters more directly into a life in ideas; a thoughtful yet colourful contemplation of the phenomena presented both from the aspect of the humanities and the sciences; a careful discrimination in the sphere of human values; the passage from ideas to ideals and the goals of life.

We have passed from the intuitive thinking of the infant years when body metabolism is most pronounced to the artistic portrayal of life in the middle years when lung and heart, the word and feeling, are most closely engaged. And finally we come to the third stage of childhood where thinking comes essentially into its own: from a limb-metabolic, to a rhythmic-circulatory, to a wakened, sense-thinking orientation in life; from intuition, by way of inspiration and imagination, to a clear intellectual grasp of phenomena. So it is we move on to the adult stage. Just as at the end of the first three years the little child says 'I', so at the end of the three stages of childhood, and with entry into adult consciousness, the 'I AM' is born.

## A threefold society

At the time of the French Revolution the call of Liberty, Equality, Fraternity resounded. Rudolf Steiner, during the calamitous years of the First World War, presented as though in answer to that call his ideas for a Threefold Commonwealth. The picture of the Threefold Commonwealth is directly parallel to that of the threefold nature of the human being as we have tried to describe it. His ideas could not be realized, and though they have given rise to study and research, and to a few modest enterprises, they remain ideas or ideals for the future. What mainly militates against them, and is likely to do so for some time to come, is the centralist trend in thought that continually seeks leadership either by individuals or through party control. Such leadership will naturally tend to impose its own stamp on development in political, economic, educational and cultural life. The twentieth century has seen a striking rise in dictatorship states, the proclaimed goal always being that of ultimate freedom. That the call for freedom has a genuine inner source in human beings today can scarcely be questioned. Yet in practice we find ourselves under pressure of increasing unfreedom. Reverting to the original call we ask: Where does freedom or liberty truly reside? Where do we expect to find equality? And though the term fraternity or brotherhood is often heard, what does it signify and where do we meet it?

Where are we to look for liberty? Essentially in the sphere of thought. We would expect every individual to be entirely free to think his own thoughts, to worship in his own style, to pursue his own cultural interest, in fact, to conduct his own cultural life untroubled and untrammeled by any question of external control.

Where shall we seek and expect to find equality? Most surely before the law. Justice belongs equally to all, before humanity and before God. That is beyond dispute. But then comes the question: What rightly belongs to humanity, what constitutes human rights? Everyone has a right to the air he breathes, to the water he drinks (why not to the bread he eats?), to education in childhood, to medical service at need, to care in old age. Whatever one might claim as rights for oneself, one would surely do in the same spirit for one's neighbour. The democratic principle is surely paramount here, in the sphere of rights. This is not the same idea as a welfare state administered from above. Rights and justice belong to the sphere of the heart, and the rulings here should spring from the heart in the mutual concern of human beings for one another.

What then do we understand by fraternity or brotherhood? One often hears the word, but where does it really live? Here we are on more difficult ground. Fraternity springs from the gifts we give through services we render for one another. This directly engages the question of work and what we mean by economic life. It is quite clear that economic and industrial life need expert leadership, but in so far as they are there not for personal gain but in service to the community on the basis of meeting actual needs, their jurisdiction involves the sphere of rights. Here things get too complex for a cursory statement. We would quote as a concrete example that Henry Adams saw as a primary evil of economic life the personal ownership of land and, along with this, any form of land speculation. Our modern life is rife with it. The corrective view would be that land should be loaned by decision of the rights sphere to those deemed competent to make the best productive use of it for the common good.

Another example might be the following. I was once asked to speak at the opening of a new school of commerce, and I stressed one point in particular. In purchasing a pair of shoes, we pay for the commodity; but there is no way we can pay for the gift or skill which enabled someone to make us shoes for our feet. We cannot traffic in human gifts, buy and sell labour, for gifts we bring with us into the world; gifts belong to the spirit; we could say that they are of God. We should not labour for money but in order to fulfil ourselves through serving others with our skills and gifts, as they through their gifts serve us. We work to sustain our fellow men even as they work to sustain us. That is how we are indebted to one another. But human needs should be a concern of the rights sphere. To work for wages determined by an employer is a form of slavery. Not to work or have the will to work (except in illness or old age) is an illness in itself, actually an evil. Not to be able to find work points to a sickness in society, an even greater evil. At every point in economic life we touch the sphere of morality, and there fraternity arises. We admit all this is difficult. It is mentioned here as a great challenge to be met, the whole question of work, wages and money.

For the present, to sum up we may say:

Liberty of thought relates to the nerve-sense system, and belongs to the cultural sphere.

Equality relates to the heart and the rhythmic system and belongs to the rights sphere.

Fraternity concerns work, production and consumption, is related to the human will and the metabolic-limb system, and belongs to the economic sphere.

Just as we live through thought, feeling and will in all three parts of the total organism, so each of us plays his part in all three spheres of the social organism. The threefold human being enters naturally into this picture of a threefold society. There need be no centralist rulership but instead a striving for a healthy interaction of all three spheres, mutually related as are the three organizations within the total single organism.

SUMMARY

| *Thinking* | *Feeling* | *Will* |
|---|---|---|
| Nerve-sense organization | Rhythmic-circulatory organization | Limb-metabolism organization |
| Cultural sphere | Rights sphere | Economic sphere |
| Liberty | Equality | Fraternity |

The subject of 'human society' can be studied from various aspects. The foregoing, growing out of the preceding descriptions, offers one such approach.

# 4
# A NEW AGE OF LIGHT

## *The age of darkness: Kali-yuga*

Ancient teachings tell of a Golden Age, Krita-yuga (20,000 years), a Silver Age, Treta-yuga (15,000 years), a Bronze Age, Dvapara-yuga (10,000 years), and a Dark or Iron Age, Kali-yuga (5000 years).

This succession of the Ages is the oriental image of the Fall, a long, protracted process of separation from the gods, in contrast to the sudden, cataclysmic event as described in the Bible. The dates given for Kali-yuga, confirmed by Rudolf Steiner, are 3101 BC to AD 1899.

It is difficult to reconcile these dates with what we know of the depth and grandeur of Egyptian culture, the wonder and the beauty of Greek culture, the birth of civil law and citizenship in Roman times, and the rise and spread of Christianity right through the Middle Ages. It is a remarkable fact though that the invention of writing in Egypt came just about the time when Kali-yuga was approaching, about 3300 BC. Until that time all culture rested on memory and the spoken word.

The succession of Ages from Golden to Silver to Bronze to Iron may be taken as symbolic of the transition in consciousness from Intuition to Inspiration to Imagination, and then to the birth of the intellectual faculty with which humanity finds itself contemplating the world from outside, no longer able to find entry into it. The way to the spirit continued to be cultivated in the Mystery Schools for the guidance of nations, but for human beings generally direct experience of higher worlds became ever more obscured.

We need only compare the vivid portrayal of life after death in the Egyptian *Book of the Dead* with the dim and shadowy Hades of the Greeks. Study confirms that with every advance in outer culture there is a corresponding diminution of active participation in the life of the spirit. In this way human experience has become more and more externalized. This reached its culmination in the nineteenth century with the advance of science and technology and, in the western world where this was taking place, the spread of scepticism towards any kind of spiritual existence.

In the case of Christianity, for example, one might have expected that two thousand years after the coming of Christ the world would have grown increasingly alive to what, if it has any meaning at all, must be regarded as the greatest of all mysteries, a God become man, to live with human beings on earth, to die a human death, in order to overcome death for man's sake. As we look down the centuries in the Christian West, what do we find?

To begin with there were those who could bear direct witness to the life of Christ Jesus, his death and resurrection. Then came the witnesses of the witnesses, and their witnesses in oral tradition. As this weakened it was succeeded by religious faith—people no longer knew but they believed through faith. Faith, as time went on, hardened into dogma. Then came a war of conflicting interpretations, and persecutions followed and heresy hunting. Then, with the advent of science, doubts arose leading to the scepticism we know.

In this context one can recall the nineteenth-century book *The Life of Jesus*, by Ernest Renan, written in all honesty and, as he believed, with good intent. He sets aside all regard for the divinity of Christ and cannot sufficiently extol the man Jesus—the simple man of Nazareth. He goes so far as to persuade himself, and through his book to persuade others, that the miracles and the resurrection were tales foisted onto the people by Jesus' followers to impress them with his greatness—strange to what extremes mistaken honesty can go.

It led on, however, to the view, the heavens having been abolished, that henceforth morality, in so far as it exists at all, is to be sought only in the human being, and that the human being must now come to terms with himself in isolation. We meet with the free-thinking nineteenth-century individualist, his words expressed in the statement, 'I hold myself responsible for thought and word and deed to myself and none other.' Historically it amounts to a declaration of moral and spiritual independence, subscribed to, also, by the pioneering scientists of that time—in itself an admirable point of departure for a new beginning. So much for the course of faith in the new scientific age.

Taking a brief glance at Christian art, selecting just a few examples, we pass from the cosmic, the lofty grandeur of a Cimabue Madonna, with a golden background of sun-filled heavenly glory, to a Fra Angelico for whom the angel world was still immediately present; then the great masters of the Renaissance who brought about, in Christian form, all the perfection of classical times, and then all the tenderness and grace of a very human Murillo Madonna, or the stern heralding of enlightenment in a Rembrandt. Then we sink away into naturalism but still for a time with the glow of the artist's sensitivity. It became impossible to develop the Madonna figure further. We are indeed alone with ourselves now in confronting the world. If anything new is to come it can only be out of the resources of our own nature—new explorations which break with all tradition. For example some would say that Turner was a master pioneer of a new life in colour.

Science also began out of a more philosophic regard for

nature. It moved from natural philosophy to natural history, and the word 'science' came later. But then, as we have seen, science chose to confine itself strictly to what the senses could offer, and to theorizing about its limited data. Eventually, amongst other discoveries of the nineteenth century, came the spectroscope, the evidence of which, combined with Newton's law of universal gravitation, led to the view that the whole visible universe was little more than an extension of the conditions found on earth. The human being himself came to be regarded as a product of the earth.

As a symptom of the times I would like to cite another interesting book, *Religion without Revelation*, by Julian Huxley, a prominent biologist. In this book Huxley explains away the Christian Trinity in what to him are the simplest terms. We are all children of nature. He identifies nature with the Father. We all have flashes of inspiration from time to time. This he takes as evidence that the evolving substance protoplasm still has life in it. These flashes represent what is otherwise described as illumination through the Holy Spirit. Then comes the third element, the capacity to relate the substance we owe to nature to the ideas that light up in us—to relate substance and idea, Father and Holy Spirit. This mediating element without which there could be no progress Huxley regards as the aspect Christians ascribe to Christ.

Huxley must be regarded as a serious, competent and honest thinker; but he has no use for any kind of personalized religion; he finds no ground in himself for considering a world beyond the senses. As a biologist he concludes that if there is to be further evolution on earth it can only be through the human being, but we must have the will to make progress, must strive to realize the best ideas we have, hence his phrase 'Evolution has grown conscious', an idea which the most pious religionist would happily share with him. Huxley retained his faith in the potential of the human being but saw that if we had nothing to strive for we would inevitably sink into apathy or despair; and thus he came to develop something akin to religion, or at least an ethics, in his humanism. We have quoted Huxley because of his uncompromising attitude where truth is concerned, and yet seemingly from his youth on an extreme reluctance and total inability to entertain any kind of thought that goes beyond the physical. He is important for he stands as evidence of a frame of mind which only our age could have produced. It poses the question: What could be the next step?

C. E. M. Joad, a teacher of philosophy early in the twentieth century, wrote *Guide to Modern Thought*. In a broad and impartial survey of the main trends of thought he speaks at one point of three dethronements: the dethronement through Copernicus of the earth from its central place in the heavens; the dethronement through Darwin of man on his planet earth; and the dethronement through behaviourist psychology of the human mind.

This still holds true, and we may well ask what has been enthroned instead. With all the severe trials of the twentieth century human life has been shaken through and through. The future continues to be uncertain and immensely threatening, and hope of outer stability is nowhere in sight. This has brought about a stirring of souls and awakening to the need for inner stability if real answers to all the many and insistent questions are to be found.

Rudolf Steiner, fully knowing and wishing to serve the positive values to be found in science, foresaw in all clarity that, with the end of Kali-yuga, a new light must dawn for humanity. Into what seems outwardly like deepening darkness, he introduced anthroposophy, a new knowledge of man, the world and human destiny, a knowledge presented in a form that makes it openly accessible. It comes as a source of new illumination from within, casting its light into all fields of new endeavour, and opening up perspectives of hope for the future.

## *The initiate teacher in the age of freedom*

An important question will almost certainly have arisen in the mind of the reader: Do we have to take what Rudolf Steiner presents as the fruits of his spiritual investigation simply on trust? Lacking his capacity and his spiritual vision, how are we to verify for ourselves the truths of which he speaks? The answer to this question can best be given in his own words:

I have often said that the facts of the spiritual world must be investigated and can be discovered only by clairvoyant consciousness; and I have often said that once someone possessed of clairvoyant consciousness has observed these facts in the spiritual world and then communicates them, they must be communicated in such a way that even without clairvoyance everyone will be able to test them by reference to the normal feeling for truth present in every soul, and by applying to them his own unprejudiced reasoning faculties. Anyone endowed with genuine clairvoyant consciousness will always communicate the facts about the spiritual world in such a way that everyone who wishes to test what he says will be able to do so without clairvoyance. But at the same time the way in which he communicates them will convey their true value and significance to a human soul.

Rudolf Steiner speaks in many places of the need for serious study of the content of anthroposophy as basic to any other inner work that one might undertake. Such study can often be difficult for we inevitably encounter in ourselves all the misconceptions and limitations of a materialistic age which have been implanted in us from our earliest years. To these we are unconsciously so habituated that it can be hard work to recognize them for what they are and to eliminate them. We will find we cannot read books on spiritual science in the same way as we read other books and still hope to benefit from them. We need to dwell on each phrase and sentence, awaiting the right feelings to meet the thoughts. Then such study will serve as an awakener, for spiritual science or anthroposophy aims to help the human being to awaken truly to himself.

Reading in this way, we may come to realize that what is offered us in the book is the one half, in order that we may awaken the other half from within ourselves in response. This becomes a real need—the internalizing of what we read and bringing it to life in ourselves. It is a common experience that re-reading something we have studied in this way lights it up for us anew almost as a discovery of our own. Thus confidence grows.

Rudolf Steiner:

What, then, does this communication and presentation of spiritual facts mean to the soul? It means that anyone who has some idea of conditions in the spiritual world can direct and order his life, his thoughts, his feelings and his perceptions in accordance with his relationship to the spiritual world. In this sense, every communication of spiritual facts is important, even if the recipient cannot himself investigate these facts with clairvoyant consciousness. Indeed, for the investigator himself these facts acquire a human value only when he has clothed them in a form in which they can be accessible to everyone. However much a clairvoyant may be able to see and investigate in the spiritual world, it remains valueless both for himself and others until he can bring the fruits of his vision into the range of ordinary cognition and express them in ideas and concepts which can be grasped by a natural sense of truth and by sound reasoning.

There is all the difference in the world between the spiritual investigator who pursues and tests his higher experiences in the true spirit of scientific research and the visionary whose impressions arise as and when they will. The Irish poet A.E. lamented the fact, at the end of his life, that he had never followed a disciplined path of meditation. We have instances when Rudolf Steiner had to wait a long time, pursuing many avenues of research, before what he was looking for might suddenly reveal itself, often where least expected. Such was the case in his search for the Grail. The answer to his search then came as an act of grace. Even so, having made his discovery and solved his problem for himself, he still had to wait until the conditions were appropriate and the right people present for communication of his findings to others. Hence his words: 'In fact, if the findings are to be of any value to himself he must first have understood them fundamentally; their value begins where the possibility of reasoned proof begins.' Only then, as he said previously, do the fruits of his work become accessible to the reasoned thinking of others, and only then can they be assimilated in freedom.

This whole question of the imparting of knowledge by the initiate to others is one Rudolf Steiner applies even to considerations beyond death.

Picture to yourselves someone who may have made quite exceptional discoveries in the spiritual world through clairvoyant observation but has never clothed them in the language of ordinary life. What happens to such a person? All his discoveries are extinguished after death; only so much remains of value and significance as has been translated into language which, in any given period, is the language expressing a healthy sense of truth.

But what is the obligation placed upon the spiritual investigator to communicate at all? Much may be at stake as to whether he does so or not. Supposing it is revealed to the spiritual investigator that humanity, in its state of ignorance, is in some great danger, is he not called on by everything holy to share what he can with his fellow human beings so that they may be rightly made aware? Here there is no compulsion, only compassion.

It is naturally of the greatest importance that clairvoyants should be able to bring tidings from the spiritual world and make them fruitful for their fellow human beings. Our age needs such wisdom and cannot make progress without it. It is essential that such communications should be made available to contemporary culture. Even if this is not recognized today [1910], in fifty or a hundred years it will be universally acknowledged that civilization and culture can make no progress unless people become convinced of the existence of spiritual wisdom and realize that humanity must die unless spiritual wisdom is assimilated ... This is true beyond a shadow of doubt. Insight into the spiritual world is absolutely essential.

Referring once again to the state after death, one can ask whether the initiate has, in fact, any advantage over someone who can only learn the truth from others. The answer is very clear. What matters above all is to possess the knowledge needed to guide one's life on earth; if one has received such knowledge and has lived by it, then that alone is what is conclusive after death. 'Whatever spiritual wisdom we have assimilated will be fruitful after death, no matter whether or not we ourselves are seers.'

This is a great moral law.

Let nobody imagine that he (the seer) gains any advantage over his fellow human beings through developing clairvoyance, for that is simply not so. He makes no progress which can be justified on any ground of self-interest. He achieves progress only in so far as he can be more useful to others. The immorality of egotism can find no place in the spiritual world. A person can gain nothing for himself through spiritual illumination. What he does gain, he can gain only as a servant of the world in general and he gains it for himself only by gaining it for others.

## *The age of light*

Rudolf Steiner left behind a great heritage of material, about thirty written works and over six thousand lectures.

Concerning the lectures he writes: 'These were really reports on lectures, more or less accurate, which, for lack of time, I could not correct. It would have pleased me best if spoken words had remained spoken words.' He had to yield to the pressure of members. At first the lectures were printed privately 'for members only', but the restriction had later to be dropped for it led to many misunderstandings.

It may be added that there is now a complete, authentic and definitive edition of the lectures running to something like three hundred volumes.

About his writings, Rudolf Steiner comments:

Whoever wishes to trace my inner struggle to set anthro-posophy before the consciousness of the present age must do this on the basis of the writings published for general circulation. Moreover, in these writings I make my position clear in relation to all striving for knowledge which exists in the present age.

And further:

I here present what took form for me more and more in 'spiritual beholding', what became the edifice of anthro-posophy—in a form incomplete, to be sure, from many points of view.

It was Rudolf Steiner's task, as a modern western initiate, to open a way for humanity out of Kali-yuga into a new age of light. Beginning with the periodical *Lucifer-Gnosis* he steadily developed his work, offering a path that passes from an exact study of natural phenomena to the spiritual facts and realities underlying them. It was for this task that his own studies and research in the nineteenth century had particularly prepared him. His work had to reach not only the open-minded thinking of trained scien-tists, but a whole age brought up to be scientifically minded. His writing especially had to be framed for this, hence he writes:

... an anthroposophical book is designed to be taken up in inner experience. Then, by stages, a form of under-standing comes about. Further deepening through exer-cises described in *Knowledge of Higher Worlds* is simply deepening confirmation. For progress on the spiritual road this is necessary; but a rightly composed anthro-posophical book should awaken the life of the spirit in the reader, not impart a certain quantity of information.

The reading of it should not be mere reading; it should be an experience with inner shocks, tensions and solutions.

At the same time, for freedom's sake, he had to obtrude on the reader as little as possible, so much so that it has been said at times that his writing seems cold, detached or dry. He himself offers the explanation:

In the matter of style, I do not write to reveal my subjective feelings in the sentences. In writing, I subdue to a dry, mathematical style what has come out of warm and profound feeling. But only such a style can have an awakening effect; for the reader must cause warmth and feeling to awaken in himself. He cannot simply allow these to flow into him from the author, leaving the clarity of his own mind obscured.

And thus the personality of Rudolf Steiner remains concealed behind his writing. The truth of what he has to say, however, can always be reached through one's own endeavour. It is only through our own labour and struggle that we begin to recognize the labour he undertook on our behalf.

What is that labour to which our own inner life has called us, other than to find our bearings in spiritual life, even as nature has placed us into physical life? With what infinite care and precision is the embryo carried from conception in the spirit to physical birth. Can the process leading to the second birth be any less caring and exact? 'The road to freedom leads through necessity'; let us follow this thought in the subsequent pages, and in its light carry further what has been said, in a preliminary way in the second chapter, in regard to the basic books.

In *Initiation and its Results*[1] we are guided to work on what
are called by an oriental name 'lotus flowers', which are astral
or soul organs of perception. The first such organ to which we
are directed is the sixteen-petalled lotus flower with eight
exercises related to it. Eight of these petals belonging to times
of natural or instinctive clairvoyance have grown dark with
the human descent from spirit into matter. We stand at the
zero point, and begin the ascent by developing the remaining
eight petals to conscious faculties of vision for the future.
They are exercises above all of watchfulness over our habits
of life.

Be watchful of your thoughts that they be truly meaningful.
Be watchful of your resolves that they be well-conceived
and well-maintained.
Be watchful of your words, that they be neither too many
nor too few, and learn to heed the words of others.
Be watchful of your outer initiatives that they be in harmony, as far as possible, with outer circumstances.
Be watchful over your own conduct in life, that you are
neither too hasty nor too tardy.
Be watchful of the high goals you set yourself that you
neither undertake what is at present beyond your capacities nor fall short of what is within them.
Be watchful in your readiness to learn from all that life
brings your way, even from a little child.
Be watchful that you maintain all the foregoing in harmonious accord with one another.

Here is a firm foundation for a beginning. Next we are led
to consider the twelve-petalled lotus flower with its corre-

---

[1] Later published as the second half of *Knowledge of Higher Worlds*
beginning with the chapter 'Some Effects of Initiation'.

sponding six exercises. These require greater effort of concentration. They carry the work to a deeper level. Whereas the previous exercises had more to do with mental perception, these may be described as being concerned with fostering greater heart perception. They again require the cultivation of certain faculties: control of thought, control of action, inner tranquillity, positivity of outlook, freedom from prejudice and prejudgement, the maintaining of the foregoing in a state of inner equilibrium.

So we move on from one lotus flower to the next, the demands increasing with each step, but always supported by the work done previously. Thus, through work and answering grace, we advance as far as our destiny allows. It is clear that such work, faithfully pursued, must lead to greater health, balance and security in inner life, and to greater ability to serve in outer life. I recall an experience I once had of climbing Snowdon in Wales at night. There were three in the party including the guide, an experienced mountaineer who knew every inch of the way. We had to follow his instructions step by step in total darkness as he led the way round protruding ridge and narrow ledge, always climbing until, with the first rays of dawn, we found ourselves creeping along a great ridge with a steep drop below. So, by degrees, we arrived at the summit, to be rewarded with a magnificent sunrise. We realized then that among the several approaches to that summit we had followed the most dangerous. But he had never faltered, and we followed with perfect trust. Along a spiritual path we surely need no lesser guidance from one who has been before. Only here it is inner rocks and boulders, declivities and obstacles that we have to surmount or circumvent.

The study of the lotus flowers and the groups of exercises connected with each of them is clearly described in the book

itself. Here we would wish to give an indication only of how
the approach to exercises can take a different form from the
one previously outlined. Each group of exercises has its own
organic unity and function in relation to that particular lotus
flower and the higher faculties to which it would ultimately
lead. It will be seen how all the exercises are directed to
developing stronger inner disciplines in the practice and
achievement of moral forces and faculties, for only these can
serve higher development.

Let us look again at the book *Theosophy*. The first chapter
describes the various members composing the human being,
those already acquired in long ages past and those to be
acquired in the course of further evolution. The ego stands as
the active agent transmuting past into future.

It is one of the wonders of anthroposophical spiritual
science that the greatest can find expression in the least, and
vice versa. Thus, once we have grasped the nature of the
threefold human being, we can recognize in him the seed
potentials related to the very highest, even to the Holy
Trinity. And, indeed, time and again, in order to understand
the smallest we have to reach out to the greatest. This is quite
particularly so in studying the human being.

In *Theosophy* we are concerned primarily with what a
person can make of himself in one life, of the consequences of
this in the life after death, and how this, in turn, conditions his
life in the following incarnation. We are guided from familiar
considerations to heights from which we can still survey the
landscape; but then we are led on into realms beyond our
conscious experience, yet maintaining all the way a sense of
reality on which we can fully rely. Thus we pass through soul
regions and spirit regions, until we return to earth once again.
How is this to be achieved without the reader, at some time,
having to abandon his sense of freedom, falling back to mere

credulity? To understand this is vital to our theme. On this point Rudolf Steiner describes his method of procedure in writing the book:

> Let it be noted how ... my theosophy is structured. Every step taken in the book is based on spiritual perception. Nothing is said which is not derived from spiritual perception; but, in graduated steps, such perception is clothed at first, at the beginning of the book, in scientific ideas, until, in rising to higher realms, it must occupy itself more and more in fully picturing the spiritual world. But this picturing grows out of a scientific approach as the blossom of a plant grows from the stem and leaves. As the plant is not seen in its entirety if it is considered only as far as the blossom, so nature is not experienced in its entirety if we do not rise from the sensible to the supersensible.
>
> So what I strove for was to set out in anthroposophy the objective continuation of science, not to place something subjective alongside science. It was inevitable that this endeavour in particular was not at first understood. Science was supposed to end with what pre-dates anthroposophy, and there was no inclination to enliven scientific ideas so as to lead to comprehension of the spiritual. People were under the spell of the habit of thought developed during the second half of the nineteenth century. They could not muster the courage to break the fetters of mere sense-perception; if they did so, they thought, they might arrive at regions where everybody asserts the validity of his own fantasy.

It has to be seen that this sense-bound thinking makes the spirit a slave to matter. It creates the illusion that truth is to be found only by further analysis of matter. This kind of thinking has filtered into our minds. It is so little born of the human spirit that it ends by negating that very spirit. Materialistic thinking is a darkening of the spirit not due to the phenomena human beings behold but to the way they behold them. The latter makes matter into the *all*, and the spirit into *nothing*. Only by overcoming this illusion inherent in materialistic thinking can the human spirit find its way out of darkness into light.

Rudolf Steiner's detached way of writing is further exemplified in his *Occult Science, an Outline*. In the opening chapter he reviews both the possible questions of the scientist and the objections that might be raised by the religious-minded. Their difficulties are taken seriously. In the second chapter a picture of the members that make up a human being are presented again. The third chapter examines sleep and death, offering a further approach to the understanding of reincarnation. Sleep is described as a younger brother of death.

> Anyone who does not continually draw strength for his weakened forces from sleep must of necessity destroy his life. Likewise, a concept of the world which is not made fruitful by a knowledge of the hidden world must lead to desolation. It is similar with death. Living beings succumb to death in order that new life may arise. It is only a knowledge of the supersensible which can shed clear light upon the beautiful words of Goethe: 'Nature created death that she might have more abundant life.'

The chapter leads us on a path through death to a new life. Then follows a mighty chapter which is the heart of the book, 'Man and the Evolution of the World'. This gives a vast panorama beginning with the dawn of world creation. It describes the successive stages in the creation of man together with all the ranks of hierarchies participating in this (see page

89 onwards). The chapter resounds like a mighty symphony for those prepared to hear it, yet it is written in a strictly formal manner.

We are led in successive cycles of time down to our own day. Chapter five is concerned with the modern path of initiation and the knowledge of man as a microcosm within the macrocosm. Then the following chapter opens a view into future stages of human and world evolution. This book was published in 1908, only six years after the first issue of *Lucifer-Gnosis*. Now, all these decades later, we can recognize what an act of courage it was to put such a book on the open market.

With regard to the use of the book and the work involved in inner schooling, we quote the following:

We need not think that it is necessary to pass through these stages successively, one after the other. On the contrary, the training may proceed in such a way, in accordance with the individuality of the student of spiritual science. He may have reached only a certain degree of perfection in a preceding stage when he begins exercises which correspond to a subsequent stage.

... The way to knowledge of supersensible worlds described here is one which every human being can follow, no matter what the situation is in which he may find himself within modern life. When describing such a path we must consider that the goal of knowledge and truth is the same in all ages of earth evolution, but that the starting points of the human being on the path have been different in different ages... The path to higher knowledge described here is eminently fit for souls who incarnate in modern times. It is one which places the point of departure for spiritual development just where the human being now stands in any situation presented by modern life.

These last words are meant to be taken quite literally. The cultivation of anthroposophy does not require withdrawal to some lonely retreat for peace and contemplation. On the contrary, one needs to learn to create for oneself moments of quiet retreat in the midst of everyday life.

It was during the time between the appearance of the *Philosophy of Freedom* in 1894 and his departure for Weimar in 1897 that Rudolf Steiner had two vital experiences which he refers to only briefly in his *Autobiography*.

To him it was clear that a true science of nature must of itself lead to a science of the spirit. What was it that infiltrated human materialistic thinking to prevent this? It was a kind of betrayal of the human spirit due to the working of certain adversary beings. In the biblical book of the Apocalypse we read of a battle between Michael and his angel host, and the Satanic hosts which were cast down to earth, where they continue to molest man and could even destroy human civilization for all time. Here is the relevant sentence:

In the thinking which can result from the science of nature—but which did not result at that time—I saw the basis upon which the human being might attain insight into the world of spirit. I laid much stress, therefore, upon the knowledge which underlies nature, which must lead to knowledge of the spirit.

Spiritually perceived there are beings for whom 'it is absolute truth that the world must be a machine', and any trend in thought that leads to such a conclusion is inspired by them.

Rudolf Steiner speaks of his 'inner struggle against the demonic powers who wanted to cause our knowledge of nature to become not perception of spirit but a mechanistic and materialistic way of thinking'. Further: *At that time I had to save my spiritual perception through inner battles. These battles formed the background to my outer experience* [author's italics].

These beings, called by Rudolf Steiner ahrimanic, can also be called spirits of darkness. It is they that have to be fought and overcome if humanity is to be led out of Kali-yuga into a new age of dawning spiritual light.

Here then is one part of the task that lay before Rudolf Steiner at that time. The other concerns our relationship to Christianity. He writes:

In this time of testing I succeeded in progressing further only when in spiritual vision I brought before my mind the evolution of Christianity.

The Christianity which I had to seek I did not find anywhere in the creeds. After the time of testing had subjected me to stern battles of the soul, I had to submerge myself in Christianity and, indeed, in the world in which the spiritual speaks thereof.

As regards his *Christianity as Mystical Fact* he writes: ... 'I included nothing in this book until I had first encountered and verified it in the spirit.' But then, what he wrote there in many ways ran counter to established doctrines. Of this struggle he writes:

The true substance of Christianity began germinally to unfold within me as an inner phenomenon of knowledge. About the turn of the century, the germ unfolded more and more. Before this turn of the century came the testing of the soul I have described. The unfolding of my soul rested upon the fact that *I had stood in spirit before the Mystery of Golgotha in most inward, most earnest solemnity of knowledge* [author's italics].

Here was the other half of his initiate task in leading out of Kali-yuga into a new future.

It is expected that the age following Kali-yuga, in which a new consciousness is to awaken in humanity, will last 2500 years. Anthroposophy states that the age predicted in the Gospel as that of Christ's second coming belongs to the same era—that within the next 2500 years humanity as a whole will experience the Christ, not in the flesh, but as Paul experienced him at Damascus. Paul had said of himself that he had come before his time. That time has arrived. This is the innermost secret and the great reality of this age of light in which we all live. Anthroposophy has come to prepare mankind for this. To behold the Christ in his second coming, we have to raise ourselves to etheric vision. That is the interpretation which anthroposophy gives to the Gospel image of Christ's coming 'upon the clouds'. We stand at the very beginning of an apocalyptic time and have inwardly to prepare to meet it, each one according to his destiny.

# 5
# MEANING IN HISTORY

## *The question*

Where shall we seek for meaning in history? That is the question we have to explore.

In today's terms we live with a big bang theory at the beginning, and a heat death theory at the end. What meaning can this offer to human history or to existence at all? Yet this is all that science has arrived at. The fact that consciousness has developed that asks the question remains an insoluble enigma.

Have the humanities more to tell us? They bring us a wide range of experiences, joys and sorrows, laughter and tears, triumphs and defeats both in inner and outer life, but all are transitory without a hint of any ultimate direction or goal. Yes, there are visionary human beings, Shakespeare with his *Tempest*, Goethe with his *Faust*, Shelley with his *Prometheus Unbound*; we rejoice to have their gifts but in the end, what more do they tell us than that 'We are such stuff as dreams are made on'. If we abide by the scientific view that is all they can possibly tell us.

Oswald Spengler's *Decline of the West* woke attention early in the twentieth century. His thesis is that a cultural period consists of a youthful era of growth and creativity, but after this reaches its peak of civilization decline ensues. He compares our present state with the decline of Rome. As for the future, we can only surmise that another dominant culture may arise as appears to have been the case in the past. Egypt, Greece, the Middle Ages each have their own distinctive character, but there is nothing to suggest continuity from the one to the other. Spengler's descriptions are of passing phenomena. Of further meaning there is no trace.

The author once asked a group of children aged 12 whom he had been telling about the life of St Francis what they thought was the difference between a legend and history. The reply came: 'The legend is more true because it tells you what history can't.' How right they were!

How was it in earlier times, before the age of modern science, when religious faith was still strong? Then human life found its meaning in ultimate union with God. The spiritual worlds were felt to be close at hand. Legends, visions, dreams, were convincing and plentiful. We may think of Joan of Arc. An untutored country girl made her way to the court of the Dauphin to tell that she had heard the voice of the archangel Michael. She was to drive the English out of France and make the Dauphin King. What concerns us here is that people believed her. She actually did lead the French to victory and forced the English to retire. The possibility of spiritual intervention through such a maid was accepted—life on earth was still felt to be guided from above. Her earthly reward was to be burnt at the stake as a witch. She held to her story to the end, a story that has fired the imagination as few have. That she heard a voice has to be credited her else there would be no story. But how many really accept the voice as a call from the archangel Michael? Joan's intervention changed the history of Europe, of France and England in particular. But that there could be such direct spiritual guidance in human affairs is something lost to our time, though it was felt to be natural only a few hundred years ago. Human history was felt to be part of a great cosmic plan. Rudolf Steiner reveals that it was indeed the archangel Michael who directed Joan and that her faith was founded on reality.

As we go further back in time, legend, vision and dream

play an ever greater part. As a further instance of this we quote the remarkable circumstances of the founding of the official Christian Church. Constantine in the fourth century AD experienced what the books describe as a 'conspicuous miracle'. On the eve of a battle with a far greater force than his own, he had a vision of a flaming cross in the sky at noon with the words 'By this conquer'. He won the battle. Later, as Emperor Constantine, in AD 324 he declared Christianity to be the official religion of the empire.

There is another significant circumstance belonging to this time. Christmas had always been celebrated on 6 January to commemorate the descent of Christ into Jesus at the Jordan baptism. As generation followed generation the under-standing of the baptism began to wane and with it the dis-tinction between the man Jesus and the divinity of Christ.

The early Church Fathers regarded the birth of Jesus as a birth in the flesh, and the event of the baptism as a birth in the spirit. It was in Constantine's time, or shortly after, that the child's birth became the traditional Christmas, and Epiphany receded into the background. Just at the point where the outer Church became firmly grounded and the persecution of the Christians ceased, the inner and greater mystery of the Christ birth grew more obscure. This kind of situation recurs continuously—an advance towards outer life and a corre-sponding dimming in inner life.

We ask: When was history as we know it—that is, as a recording of outer events—first born? This leads back to Herodotus, the acclaimed father of history. He lived in the fifth century BC. It is astonishing to think that history as we know it is only two thousand five hundred years old. The world of myth and legend was still abundantly rich in the Greek soul, though in a lessening degree. Herodotus, a great traveller, wrote out of his own varied life experience. He was a type of modern man in his day. Thus history from its beginning is concerned with the contemporary and transient rather than the eternal.

We have already referred to the fact that writing goes back no further than to Egypt, about 3300 BC. Those early inscriptions on monuments and temple walls tell of the dynasties, the customs of the people, but all is pervaded still with a sense of the spiritual mysteries underlying outer life. Rudolf Steiner tells us that the first writing was born as direct vision of the spiritual was dying out. It is interesting to note that Kali-yuga also began at this time. Divorced from the spirit, history becomes an empty vessel. Without the spirit what real meaning can history have? Spiritual science was born just as Kali-yuga ended, kindling a new light for the understanding of life and destiny on this earth.

To begin with we face a double dilemma. Looking out-wards we are persuaded by science to identify ourselves with matter, and looking inwards, to merge our being with the animal world of instincts. Either way we are lost to ourselves.

Thus Rudolf Steiner faced a double task: on the one hand to free science from materialism, on the other to reveal to man his true source of being. Science has sought for the infinit-esimal particle from which to develop its notion of the world. Spiritual science or anthroposophy, in contrast, takes its start from the universal realm of divine being and descends, stage by stage, in the story of creation.

Christ, walking as man on earth, said to his disciples: 'I am the Alpha and the Omega', the beginning and the end. In so far as human beings can also say 'I am', what part do we have in that statement by Christ? His words tell us we are in a tran-sitional stage between coming into being and passing away. He said, 'I am with you always even unto the end of the world,' and he also said, 'Heaven and earth will pass away but my word will not pass away.' How do we participate in the living word? How have we arrived at what we are? What is our responsible role in the present? What opens up for us as future?

## Cosmic background

Turning once again to chapter four in *Occult Science, an Outline*, we are asked to make a prodigious leap in imagination to very elevated states of being. If we are prepared to take this leap in thought and imagination, there opens up an immense saga of events succeeding one another, including all the hierarchical beings of antiquity, still known to Aristotle and to early Christianity. Stage by stage we learn to see how the history of man and his world are invested with profoundest meaning, how the present human state and that of the world become ever more understandable, and what real tasks and challenges meet us for the future. A view opens up that calls on us to proceed step by step, not only as earthly beings possessed of mind and conscience, but as spiritual and immortal natures assigned a role in the great goals of human and world evolution. We learn that in the whole history of the world from the dawn of creation to the present moment nothing is unrelated. So, too, we learn to see the world of nature around us including the human being as one integral whole in which no single feature stands alone. Only in so far as the world grows to a unity of past, present and future can human life gather meaning and purpose. The law of each for all and all for each becomes abundantly clear, not as an externally imposed law, as was the case when humanity was still in its childhood, but as the law of one's innermost being ever since Christ, moving amongst us, said, 'I am come to fulfil the law.' What was once conformity to outer law has now become a path of inner fulfilment.

Our consideration of the four elements, fire, air, water, earth will have helped prepare us for this journey through chapter four of *Occult Science*. We have seen how these elements are related to man in his fourfold constitution of ego, astral body, etheric body and physical body, and how through the elements of air, water and earth the kingdoms of animals, plant and mineral are gathered around him. Now looking to the body of the earth as a whole, that too consists of the four elements: an independent zone of warmth, the thermosphere; the atmosphere; the hydrosphere including the mists and vapours; and lastly the lithosphere, the mineral rock. We are accustomed to see these as separate zones. It is possible, however, to consider the earth as an organic whole: a physical body of rocks; an encircling life of plants; a sentient life in the animals; and finally human consciousness as also intrinsic to nature. There was a time when the earth was felt to be a mother, when people would prostrate themselves out of love for Mother Earth. The earth and its kingdoms are one. The earth in its wholeness embodies form, life, soul and consciousness. Perceived in this way, the planet earth becomes a being in its own right, a heavenly body, maintained by an 'intelligence' uniquely its own. Even in the late Middle Ages people spoke of the *intelligences* of the heavenly bodies and the harmony of the spheres.

Truly we need to learn to love the earth; the steadfast strength of its rocks, the flowing rhythmic life of its plants, the joy in motion of its animals, the contemplative depth of human awareness, the earth as habitat of all this vast variety with its resplendent and manifold beauties. The astronauts, beholding it from space, were filled with wonder at its beauty as a heavenly body, their planetary home. Beyond all that is the mystery of its movement around its own axis, making day and night, and its orbital flight bringing the wondrous round of the seasons. There may begin to awaken in us subtler feelings and impressions such as the sages had of old, in seeing the earth in all its manifestations as the handiwork of a world of divine beings. We, today, have to struggle to rid ourselves of the spectre of the earth as a spinning top of inert matter carrying an accidental life upon its surface.

In the spiritual worlds there are beings, relationships between beings, and activities arising through these relationships. What we regard as outer objects in nature are manifestations of such hidden workings. Where today's science speaks of masses and energies, spiritual science speaks of the will and substance of beings. There is no outer nature unrelated to living, spiritual beings. Asked whether the heavenly beings have ideals comparable to the ideals of human beings, Rudolf Steiner replied that the human being is their ideal, in his continual evolving. In so far as they participate in our evolution, they carry their own evolution forward. Thus they have their own destinies and yet form an integral part of human destiny.

Nothing is more intimate and exalted than to discover that, as threefold beings, we are directly related to the Holy Trinity, to the will of the Father, the love of the Son, the light of the Holy Spirit. The hierarchical beings have been known in the mystery schools from all time. They compose the three-times three choirs of angels. The following are their names:

|  | *Greek* | *Christian* | *Spiritual Science* |
|---|---|---|---|
| Beings of the first hierarchy | Seraphim<br>Cherubim<br>Thrones | Seraphim<br>Cherubim<br>Thrones | Seraphim<br>Cherubim<br>Spirits of Will |
| Beings of the second hierarchy | Kyriotetes<br>Dynamis<br>Exusiai | Dominions<br>Mights<br>Powers | Spirits of Wisdom<br>Spirits of Movement<br>Spirits of Form |
| Beings of the third hierarchy | Archai<br>Archangeloi<br>Angeloi | Principalities<br>Archangels<br>Angels | Spirts of Personality<br>Archangels<br>Angels |

Above these beings in their ascending glories is the Trinity they serve.

We may now, in briefest survey, give the main outlines of chapter four of *Occult Science.*

The earth as we know it passed through three previous conditions or, more accurately, through three earlier planetary incarnations, to arrive at its present state.

The first of these came about through the deeds of sacrifice of exalted beings named Thrones or Spirits of Will. They, having reached fulfilment in their own evolution at the stage they had then attained, gave freely of their own substance to provide the ground for another, a new evolution, that of the human being. The substance thus offered was outer physical warmth born of an inner gift of love. This constituted the first beginning of external creation. Within the manifold streams of warmth, as described, were laid down the germinal seeds of what, after aeons of time, were to become today's physical bodies.

There can be no greater contrast than this description of an all-encompassing world of warmth at the beginning as sacrificial deed and the modern physicist's view of a universal spiritless heat death at the end.

It is typical of anthroposophy to find connections between what is nearest and what seems most remote. For instance, the intimate relationship between will and warmth is immediately understandable: every exercise of energy or will releases its measure of warmth. But further than that, the warmth we bear within us, our blood warmth, determines our balance of health and our very life; yet how that warmth is generated and how maintained, and how physical warmth relates to moral warmth are questions that remain far from common explanation. It is also a remarkable fact that our body warmth of 98.4°F is well above the temperature of our rooms, normally set for comfort at 68–70°F; we thus carry a warmth body of our own, distinct from the environment. It is thus not too difficult to conceive of a link between the warmth within us and the warmth at the dawn of creation.

Greek mythology speaks of that age as the age of Chronos. Out of timelessness was born time which set the course for human evolution until its culmination when time will again cease to be. Beyond the physical germs, the life, soul and spirit of the human being rested in the divine. At the end of this great cosmic age, all that had so far been created was drawn back into a state of purely spiritual existence called *Pralaya*— a state bearing comparison with our passage through the spiritual worlds between successive incarnations.

Then all re-emerged at a more advanced stage, and into the work of outer creation there now streamed the sacrificial deeds and substance of the Kyriotetes, the Dominions or Spirits of Wisdom. The first creation was one of outer darkness. Now there was born the world of light and with it the creation of space. As one can speak of inner and outer warmth, so, too, of inner and outer light, inner and outer space, the one aspect more inward and spiritual, the other more outward and physical. As this primordial light radiated through the previously created warmth, the latter underwent a partial condensation into air, not yet air as we know it, yet giving rise to a kind of pulsation, mirroring life. The physical germs were thus endowed with a quality of life. The air can be regarded as the shadow aspect of the light, a difficult conception from a modern perspective.

In these descriptions we must imagine that we are dealing with measureless aeons of time, with cosmic dimensions. There came a second Pralaya followed by the third stage of creation. To the deeds of the Spirits of Will and the Spirits of Wisdom were added the gifts and the workings of the Spirits of Movement. Into Creation there entered the world of tone, harmony, dynamic relationships through movement. This finds reflection in our world of music, but also in all matters of ratio and proportion that rule in substance, in the secret workings of chemistry, for example. Thus in a higher sphere, beyond warmth there is engendered light, and beyond light tone, while below, warmth condenses into air and air further into the fluid nature of water—the water that lives in colour, chemistry and life. Substance had arrived at an organic consistency resembling horn but had not yet mineralized further. Corresponding to the three elements, warmth, air and water, Rudolf Steiner describes three intermediary kingdoms, mineral-plant, plant-animal, and animal-man. As spiritual being the human being had not yet finally descended but, still from divine heights, shone down upon the physical, etheric and astral natures below. There were now sentient forms possessed of elementary nerve, sense, respiratory, circulatory and digestive organs.

And now this vast complexity of life and being withdrew into a further Pralaya to emerge finally, stage by stage, as our present planet earth. It was the Exusiai, the Spirits of Form, the Elohim of the Old Testament, who now let their powers stream into the world to shape it further, reaching through warmth, air and water to the mineral rocks, the fourth element, earth. This rock is the floor of the world on which the human being was finally to descend to pursue his destiny in growing awareness of his own identity. Here on earth, through our own waking consciousness and directed will, we need ultimately to establish our own relationship with the hierarchies that begot us.

Drawing on earlier sources, Rudolf Steiner named the earth's previous planetary incarnations: Ancient Saturn, Ancient Sun and Ancient Moon. These are not to be confused with the bodies bearing the same names in our solar system.

## *The present earth*

When the earth emerged from Pralaya it had to recapitulate the earlier conditions to reach its present stage. Spiritual science tells of a Polarian age of warmth, a Hyperborean age of warmth and air, a Lemurian age of warmth, air and water; and then how in Atlantean times the fourth element came into being making the final condition of warmth, air, water and earth as described earlier. It was only then, with depositing of solid mineral substance, that the human being could finally assume his vertical shape though this had been partly prepared for in late Lemuria. The composition of the human body was still pliable and largely fluid and could therefore dissolve away without leaving any trace in the rocks. That is why geology has failed to find any fossil form that could have been the direct ancestor of present man. The reverse is in fact the case: the primitive fossil types represent a premature descent and fixation into densifying matter. In this we may recognize the law of restraint ruling in human development to which reference has already been made. The human form was present as conception from the beginning but was the last to reach full outer manifestation. We may imagine this ideal form very slowly descending into substance, and answering, ascending forms being arrested while the central stream carrying humanity forward could continue to evolve further. Le Comte de Noüy in his *Human Destiny* goes so far as to describe the animal kingdom as the debris of human development.

It follows that the existing rocks of the earth, though they, too, form a sequence in line with that of the great earth stages, must all have appeared only in the course of Atlantean times. Rudolf Steiner describes them as merely reflecting at a much later time what had gone before. This is shown in the following table.

WITHIN ATLANTEAN TIMES

| | | |
|---|---|---|
| The Azoic Age | as yet no fossils | a reflection of Polaria |
| The Palaeozoic Age | showing early life forms up to fishes and coal flora | a reflection of Hyperborea |
| The Mesozoic Age | with a great increase in fossil types up to reptiles | a reflection of Lemuria |
| The Kainozoic Age | with more recent and advanced fossils up to mammals and modern flora | a reflection of Atlantis itself |

The most recent rocks of all since the last glacial age, 10,000 BC, are described as containing 'The Age of Man'.

This indicates how the human being as we know him was the *last* to descend to the earth though the first to be conceived at the very dawn of creation.

In imagination we may look back to a time when Adam and Eve arose as human prototypes. In consciousness they still were in a paradisial state of innocence surrounded by ethereal glory. Then came the event of the Temptation and Fall in late Lemuria. This brought a rude awakening through Lucifer out of a state of blissful innocence. They found themselves stripped bare—'naked and ashamed'. At the same time their consciousness of the heavens and God was darkened so that they felt 'cast out' of paradise into a world of labour and of pain. This marked the birth of earthly human history. Yet the human being stepped into this history uniquely as an upright being. By mid-Atlantis he had acquired the utterance of linguistic sounds as distinct from the natural cries of other creatures. By the end of Atlantis he could experience the first beginnings of thought and an incipient sense of self. What the child of today achieves in the first three years of life, it took humanity many thousands of years to attain. Rudolf Steiner gives a vivid description of this in his book *Atlantis and Lemuria* (also published under the title *Cosmic Memory*). All through this time the spiritual guidance of mankind was maintained through Mystery

Schools, conducted at first by divine beings, and later, in course of time, by the most advanced and elevated members of the human race.

The destruction of Atlantis and the sinking of that continent below what is now the Atlantic Ocean covers a period of time which led to great migrations eastwards, and some also to the west. We see how the ancient cultures of Peking and Peru show features of common origin. The floods following the time of the glacial epoch find an account not only in the Old Testament but in widespread legends amongst early peoples.

A new era was to come, that of the post-Atlantean cultures, of which the present one is the fifth (with a sixth and seventh to follow), before the earth goes through its next cataclysmic change. The essential character of this post-Atlantean time is expressed in our progressive awakening to selfhood.

## The post-Atlantean cultural epochs

The table that follows shows our modern epoch as having begun in AD 1413 and the preceding one, the Graeco-Roman, in 747 BC, an interval of 2160 years between the one and the other. Further, the modern age comes under the astrological sign of the Fishes, the previous one under the sign of the Ram. A similar span of time is allotted to each of the earlier epochs, each under its own constellation: for Ancient Egypt the Bull; for Ancient Persia the Heavenly Twins, Castor and Pollux; for Ancient India Cancer. Going further back we reach, with Leo, the final phase of Atlantis. If we follow the round of the zodiac through all twelve constellations this covers an era of twelve times 2160 or 25,920 years, a Platonic Year.

What underlies this is the fact that the solar and the stellar day are not identical. The sun always falls back a little. Since the year is reckoned from sunrise at the spring equinox, the direction of the sun in relation to the zodiac shifts a little each year by what is known as the equinoctial precession. This means that the sun moves from one constellation to the next, in this way making a complete round of the zodiac in the course of a Platonic Year.

In earlier times, right up to the end of the Middle Ages, the sun, moon, planets and stars were felt to be one great cosmic community, with the human being as a microcosm within this macrocosm. The sun was regarded as regent of the heavens, the spiritual as well as the physical source of light and life. Its position in relation both to the heavens and the earth was then one of paramount importance—a past wisdom which is lost to modern humanity.

The historical cultural epochs as shown do not tally with the astronomical epochs which always fall earlier by as much as two or three centuries and vary in length according to the sizes of the constellations. These astronomical figures, accurate as outer measurements, show no discernible connection with the dates for the culture epochs presented in our historical survey.

The historical cultural epochs as described by Rudolf Steiner follow an inner path. The hope, as for all genuine scientific exploration, is that these two modes of perceiving the world may one day meet to confirm and render each other fruitful.

That is certainly the aim and direction of spiritual science, that spirit and matter, inner and outer, will one day be perceived each as a revelation of the other.

| Epoch | Dates | Zodiacal sign | |
|---|---|---|---|
| Modern epoch | AD 1413–AD 3573 | Fishes | Pisces |
| Graeco-Roman epoch | 747 BC–AD 1413 | Ram | Aries |
| Ancient Egyptian epoch | 3907 BC–747 BC | Bull | Taurus |
| Ancient Persian epoch | 5067 BC–3907 BC | Twins | Gemini |
| Ancient Indian epoch | 7227 BC–5067 BC | Crab | Cancer |

It will be obvious that there must be much overlapping of the epochs—nothing begins and ends abruptly, but the above table can serve as a broad guide. If we go further back by the same kind of reckoning, we arrive at the sign of the Lion, Leo, in Atlantis.

Towards the end of Atlantis, then, humanity was still in its early infancy. Another way of expressing it might to be say that humanity was still closely wrapped in the spiritualities, which means also that only the very highest powers, the gods themselves, and later the greatest of human initiates could provide the education and culture of the people of that time.

We cannot in this series include Chinese culture in the post-Atlantean cultures because in its spiritual origin it leads back to those high sources which pervaded Atlantis itself. Even the language is totally different from the Sanskrit of Ancient India, from which have descended most of our western languages with their cultures.

Anthroposophy describes how in Atlantis there were Mystery Schools or Oracles guided by the intelligences of the planetary spheres. Greatest of these was the Sun Oracle, ruled and guided by the being we call today the archangel Michael. When the migrations began, the great initiate of the Sun Oracle led a company of his closest disciples eastwards to a region in western Asia. From that supersensible spiritual centre impulses emanated for the founding of the successive cultural epochs as shown in the preceding table.

## Ancient India

The culture of Ancient India was guided by the Seven Holy Rishis. Rudolf Steiner describes them as simple persons in daily life, but when they were together at certain times they were totally transfigured. They were lifted up to the most exalted

heights whence they brought back the wisdom needed to guide
the people. The present *Rig-veda*, with all the sacred quality of
its verses, gives but the faintest echo of their sublime teachings.

Another source of guidance for the Indian people was that
of the beloved Krishna whose legendary life is celebrated in
song and dance each year. He descends in times of great
spiritual need as an Avatar, a messenger of the god Vishnu. It
is thus we meet him in the *Bhagavadgita*, the Song of Songs, as
charioteer to the hero Arjun. There is to be a battle between
kith and kin, a dreadful thing to contemplate since the blood
bond was held to be the most sacred of all. Arjun shrinks back
from his ordeal. Krishna teaches Arjun of reincarnation, that
death to the body is not death to the soul, and that when a
higher destiny calls we have to obey. In this teaching we may
recognize the beginning of what is much later to meet us in the
teachings of Christ, leading out of community based on
natural inheritance and the blood to community in the spirit.

An outstanding feature of Indian life is the perpetuation of
the ancient caste system which nevertheless is wholly bound
to the blood and the circumstances of birth. There the only
consoling factor is the teaching of repeated earth lives.
Buddha abolished caste in his teaching in the sixth century BC
but it still rules in Hindu India. Mahatma Gandhi, who strove
so nobly to retrieve the situation of the Pariahs, calling them
the Children of God, himself remained a faithful Hindu.

We meet in the caste system in a spiritual and cultural form
the reality of the four elements descending from fire, to air, to
water, to earth. At all times 'fire' is the holiest element, the
element of highest love, devotion and sacrifice. So it is that
the highest caste is that of the Brahmins, the priestly teachers
who alone have access to the secret doctrine. Next below them
are the Kshatriyas, the caste of the warriors, princes, rulers.
The Brahmins teach them through the sacred books how to

rule their dominions, the spaces they command, by adherence to the will of the gods. Below the Kshatriyas are the Vaisyas, described as merchants, sometimes as artisans. They are the voyagers and travellers, carrying the necessities of life from one region to another—representing the circulating waters that sustain daily life. Last and humblest of all are the Sudras, most bound to the earth; yet each caste has its virtues and its ideal, and their particular virtues are patience, endurance and trust in the high ruling of destiny.

The great longing in this first post-Atlantean culture was to reach back to the divine, the memory of which still lived on powerfully in human souls. Therefore the world of outer nature was still felt to be alien at that time, giving no sense of home, hence the term *maya*—usually translated as illusion. The illusion lay in imagining that there could be anything of abiding value in this transient earth existence.

Sanskrit, as stated earlier, is the origin of most of our western languages. A highly cultured Indian, a scientist, once asked me: 'Why is it that when I read a line of Sanskrit I feel as though transported into a state of ecstasy, whereas the finest English poetry does not move me in that way.' The fact is, as described by Rudolf Steiner, that in the ancient languages the very sounds of the words quicken a sense of divine presence which is no longer possible to later language. The fact that Sanskrit is the mother and source of subsequent cultures makes an immediate bond between them so that they succeed one another, different though they are, somewhat like the succeeding phases in a human lifetime.

## Ancient Persia

Unlike India, in Ancient Persia spiritual guidance rests with one great individuality, Zarathustra, or Zoroaster, the golden star. Rudolf Steiner has much to tell about him though there seems little or no evidence that he ever existed. Yet there are many notable legends about him.

One legend tells that Zarathustra dwelt in a cave high up a mountain from which he daily gazed upon the sun. There he beheld Ahura Mazda, the great Aura, the Sun within the sun, radiating light and life through all the world. A further legend tells that there was once revealed to him a vision of this being, later named the Christ, enthroned with Eagle, Lion, Bull and a Human Form around him. He had the foreknowledge that this being would eventually descend to earth.

The direction Zarathustra gave to culture was the very opposite of that of Ancient India. He taught love for the earth. He derived from the stars the calendar whereby to guide life according to the seasons. He introduced irrigation and agriculture. He taught that one of the most sacred places on earth was where the animal gave its droppings to the soil. He transformed the wolf into the faithful dog. Home and family were holy.

Zarathustra portrayed life as a great battle between Ahura Mazda or Ormuzd, the god of light, and Ahriman, the god of darkness, a battle that, at that time, was fought by higher powers around the human being who was still in his evolutionary infancy. Whereas the Indian teaching led the soul up to the heights, the teaching of Zarathustra was to lead the soul down so that the human being might learn to know himself as a true denizen of the earth.

The *Zend-Avesta* which, like the *Rig-veda*, was written down a long time later, contains a characteristic verse, a prayer to the beings who inspire good thoughts, good words, good deeds for protection against the beings who inspire evil thoughts, evil words, evil deeds.

## Ancient Egypt

The Egyptian epoch comes far more within the scope of accessible knowledge. Rudolf Steiner revealed that Zarathustra had two intimate pupils to whom he imparted very special gifts derived from his own nature. The one was Thoth-Hermes, the founder of Egyptian culture, the other Moses, the law-giver. The former could teach out of the wisdom of the stars; the latter out of the mysteries of time. Both, in their very different ways, were preparing for the coming of Christ who would say 'I am come to fulfil the law'. In both of these cultures, the human being's soul-spiritual nature had entered more deeply into bodily incarnation, so that human life and human relationships acquired more of an individual character. Evidence of this deeper descent into matter may be seen in the fact that Egyptian culture is much occupied with death and the mystery of death.

The myth of the descent of Osiris, a sun being, to the earth, of how he is slain and dismembered into fourteen parts by his dark brother Typhon (Seth), of how Isis his moon bride wanders through all the land to find these parts, how for each part she raises a temple; how Osiris, an immortal, returns to heaven; how he there sits enthroned in the judgment seat where the dead, each one with his own secret Osiris within him, approach him, the great Osiris on his throne; of the scales for the weighing of souls used by Thoth-Hermes, and the apportioning of destiny—this tremendous picture from the *Book of the Dead* penetrates the whole of Egyptian life. It carries in it a foreshadowing of One who would actually suffer death in the flesh and achieve a resurrection promising new life to the human being. The great *Book of the Dead*, though treating death with all the awe attendant to it, nevertheless presents it as a passage to a new life.

We have already referred to the sleep-death ordeal of initiation. The Pharoah was expected to be so initiated. The pyramid was in effect a tomb for the soul to rise heavenwards, transcending the weight of matter below. On the other hand the strange practice of embalming the dead had the effect of holding the discarnate soul close to the earth as though to draw it more deeply into matter, so that in later lives it might develop a consciousness more related to the earth. Our modern materialism is not disconnected from this. But the sense of the spiritual in all life was still very strong. The Nile was a sacred river descending from a divine source to provide, through agriculture, people's daily bread. Agriculture and medicine progressed into real arts, and art itself played a great part in ceremonial living, as is plentifully illustrated in the works left behind. Yet in the figure of the Pharaoh, sitting with his legs apart, hands on knees, his eyes gazing as though into infinity, birds like messengers from afar whispering secrets into his ears, we recognize that consciousness was still felt to stream in from realms beyond earth.

We have yet to consider the great enigmatic figure of the Sphinx, raised above the sands, calling on us even now as it did then to solve the riddle of our own existence. There it stands, silent now, though legend tells there were times when it emitted sounds. A great imaginative power impressed it with the four apocalyptic beasts so vividly described three thousand years later in the Book of Revelation, yet already forevisioned by Zarathustra, and here united into one mighty form: the great wings of the eagle, the powerful chest of the lion, the fiery force of the bull; and then the human countenance, presaging the threefold human being not yet manifest. The Sphinx of Egypt gazes into a future when the archetypal human being will stand openly revealed—*Ecce Homo*!

## Ancient Greece

And now, moving forwards in time again, we come to the Graeco-Roman, the fourth cultural epoch. This epoch extended to the end of the Middle Ages, but it is Greece we need particularly to consider in terms of advancing human consciousness. We can only select a few significant features from the epics, the dramas and the philosophy. Greece opens up a totally new chapter in man's experience of himself and the world.

In the *Iliad* the two outstanding figures are Hector and Achilles. They epitomize, by their different natures, the characters of the opposing armies. Achilles is of the younger race, the Greek, violent in his love and hate, able to sulk when offended, but in action moving with a proud impetuosity that nothing can restrain. Because he felt wronged by Agamemnon he refused to accompany his beloved friend Patroclus into battle, but then when he heard that Patroclus had been killed by a death blow from Hector, his rage against Hector knew no bounds. Hector belonged to an old race, depicted in the figure of aged Priam, his father. Hector is as valiant as Achilles, but wise and forbearing. He moves forward with quiet resolve, prepared to look destiny in the face despite forebodings of death. He is killed by Achilles whom nothing else would satisfy but that his body should be thrown to the dogs to be mutilated by them and torn apart. Only the kneeling figure of Priam is able to dissuade him.

But now, there is a background to this battle of the two heroes. The gods are active in it, Apollo on behalf of Hector, and Pallas Athene, determined that Achilles must win. Their fate has been decided already by decree of Jove. In the narrative Pallas Athene actually fools Hector so that he loses his guard. In the end then it is a duel between Apollo, a sun being, and Pallas Athene sprung from the brow of Jove. It is her mission to foster a new force of intelligence. She is the inspirer of the Greek art of philosophy. The warm heart of Apollo pleading for Hector has to give way. The old must die that the new may be born. By confronting a dying culture the Greeks, impetuous, virile, young, come to a new stage of consciousness out of which to mould their future. Helen for whom they fought is the embodiment of the beauty that will shape their art. The Trojans, in encountering the youthfulness of the Greeks, though defeated in battle, receive an impulse of renewed life which, through Aeneas, will flow into shaping the future of Rome. Human beings are still agents who fulfil the will of gods and not yet fully themselves.

The whole of the Trojan War which is part mythical, part historical, rages around the figure of Helen of Troy. According to the legend, Paris, a son of old Priam and brother of Hector, had actually abducted her from Greece where she belonged. Her beauty, renowned through all time since, is semi-divine in character, expressing all beauty in nature and in human creativity. It is for this that the Greeks fought. Paris hoped she would be the means of renewing the life and culture of dying Troy. For the Greeks she was to be the embodiment of all that was to flower as beauty in Greek art and culture. Hence they were to be called Hellenes, and Greek art, Hellenic Art.

Here is an example of how the tales of antiquity carry within them a depth of meaning far beyond mere logic and reason. So, too, Pallas Athene, who sprang into being from the forehead of Jove, was the embodiment of the new faculty of thought as Greek philosophy, hence the city of Athens is named after her, and to be an Athenian meant to be specially endowed with the gift of her being. All the Greek heroes and heroines, including the divine Apollo, bore something of this divine or semi-divine character.

The nearest term we have in modern usage may be in the word genius. Amongst its several meanings, the *Oxford English Dictionary* includes: supernatural being, exalted intellectual power, instinctive and extraordinary, creative and inventive capacity.

What we are attempting in this brief survey of the cultural epochs is to capture a sense of how the faculty of imagination or spiritual vision changed from epoch to epoch.

Ulysses is the third main figure in the *Iliad*. He is described as *cunning*. By the subterfuge of the wooden horse, the Trojans are lured out of the fastness of their city walls to their downfall. This same Ulysses or Odysseus, is the hero of the *Odyssey*. There we see his intelligence take other forms. We see him embarking on a voyage of perilous adventures; he passes through the dangers of Scylla and Charybdis; by a cunning ruse he defeats the one-eyed Cyclops that would devour him; he escapes the beguiling singing of the Sirens, and overcomes the witchery of Circe. He crosses the dread River Styx to reach at last the bournes of Hades and have communion with the dead, bringing back from there new sources of guidance for the living. He returns a wanderer in disguise to his home, in fact a new man, to disperse the crowd of lying aspirants, the hungry lusts and passions that assail his consort Penelope who, by her courage, faith and constancy, no lesser trials than his, had held the way open for his return as initiate guide to his people. In this wondrous tale of initiation we recognize the far-seeing inner vision of 'blind Homer'.

In connection with Greek drama we will confine ourselves to the theme of Orestes. The following are the circumstances. Agamemnon, to appease the angry waves which threatened

his ships on the way to Troy, sacrificed his daughter Iphi-
genia. After ten years he returns home a victor, but Clytemnestra, his wife, in revenge for the death of their daughter, has
him murdered. Orestes, their son, is on a journey. Suddenly
he is confronted by the furious Erinnyes, the shades of his
dead father, demanding revenge on their part. Bound by the
old law, he has no other recourse. He returns home and brings
about the death of his mother. But now it is her shades that
pursue him, giving him no peace. Where is he to go? He flees
to the temple of Pallas Athene, pleading for her intervention
on his behalf. Whose is the guilt? That is the question to be
resolved. The shades of Clytemnestra will not be appeased
and demand vengeance. Apollo appears and a dialogue
ensues between him and Pallas Athene. Again these two gods
confront each other as opposites, the former defending the
old law of retribution, of pity for the victim, the latter with
her philosophic vision intent on finding a new resolution. In
the end she invites twelve citizens of Athens to form a court of
justice. Apollo and Pallas Athene plead their causes. The
citizens' votes divide equally. Then Pallas Athene, since
Orestes had sought help in her temple, gives the casting vote
in his favour. The unending era of tragedy following tragedy
is broken. Orestes is set free. A new day has dawned. The
fearful, aged Erinnyes are transformed into beautiful temple
maidens singing a new song of hope and harmony for the
future.

Many years ago I produced a version of this play with older
students at the New York Rudolf Steiner School. The effect of
the final scene was deeply moving. It was like a premonition of
the resurrection scene at Easter, the weight of death overcome
and a new life begun. This was the work of Aeschylus.

Euripides, his younger contemporary, wrote a drama on
the same theme. Already the supersensible element is more

veiled. In Euripides's version Orestes is no longer pursued by spectres. Instead, he is lying on a couch in torment, attacked from within. Rudolf Steiner draws attention to the fact that here we have the actual moment of the birth of conscience. What had been experienced clairvoyantly from outside has vanished to become interiorized as conscience, and this profound change takes place within the lifetime of an older and a younger contemporary.

Perhaps the greatest innovation in Greek culture is the birth of philosophy, a word combining love and wisdom. With the entry of philosophy we have reached a stage in human progress when the older pictorial consciousness withdraws. In its place come the thoughts to which we are accustomed, but thoughts endowed with life, so that the world of ideas is a real world in which we are at home. We may recall the death scene of Socrates. Some of his closest disciples were with him when the attendant entered with the poison he was to take. He had been condemned, accused of misleading the young and drawing them away from the old gods. Actually he was trying to wean them from relying in their judgements on mere instinct and inborn habits. Having taken the poison, he continued with his calm discourse, remarking at one point that the cold was creeping up his limbs and would presently reach the heart. Some who were present wept. Socrates reproved them gently. Did they not yet realize that throughout life the philosopher is striving to die to the allurements of the world of the senses in order to reach the realm of immortal values, the realm of ideas? Why then weep because he is leaving for the home he has sought for all through life.

For Plato, for Socrates, the world of ideas is also the world of ideals. Thus Socrates taught of the four great ideals or virtues, wisdom, justice, courage, temperance, most remarkably the same ideals that had taken outer form in the caste system of India thousands of years before. What had once given rise outwardly to a great social structure was now reborn ideally from within. In such a transition from outer to inner guidance we begin to sense the true meaning of human history.

Aristotle carried experience a stage further. He sought for the idea in its outer manifestation in nature. This established him as the guiding spirit in science for two thousand years. He was still able to see the outer world with inner perception. For those who lack that inner eye, Aristotle, as scientist, is wholly discredited. Galileo rejected him utterly.

Aristotle was the teacher of Alexander the Great, born the night that the Mystery Centre at Ephesus was destroyed by an act of arson. Rudolf Steiner describes it as a wonderful esoteric school for men and women alike. The teachings given there related much to the mystery of the word as though in preparation for the greatest mystery to come—'and the Word was made flesh and dwelt among us'. By the time of Alexander, spiritual knowledge was already much on the wane. His mission was not outer conquests as is often supposed, but to establish centres where knowledge of the divine could be resuscitated. There was great emptiness of soul everywhere. There is a legend about Caesar Augustus, the greatest of the Caesars. He was about to be deified by his people when he saw a vision of a child born in Bethlehem, the King of Kings. Paul in the Acts describes how he and Barnabas were hailed as the returned Mercury and Jupiter. On Paul denying this, the people there were so enraged that the two barely escaped being stoned to death. To such a low ebb had life in the spirit sunk.

The fourth post-Atlantean cultural epoch covers an immense range of events: the rise of Christianity; the decline of Rome; the rise of Islam; the Crusades; the great monastic schools; the great cathedrals; the mediaeval walled cities; Church supremacy, the feudal system, and the ensuing struggle between Church and State; the Troubadours; the mediaeval guilds; the miracle and mystery plays at the Christian festivals; folklore and song and dance—and so much else. Yet with all these changes, human beings looked to the stars as to the homes of heavenly intelligences, and felt the earth to be the centre of it all. The Ptolemaic view of the world ruled everywhere. Thus there was a common ground of outlook from Homer to Dante—they stood at opposite ends of a single epoch. By contrast, from Dante to Copernicus, with little more than a century between, the change of outlook was startlingly great. The world was turned upside down. It is that change that brings us to the fifth post-Atlantean epoch in which we now are.

## The fifth epoch

Beginning from 1413, when the sun first entered the constellation of the Fishes, we are still, as an epoch, very young, with fifteen hundred years more to go. Obedience, whether to Church or State, had been the prevailing rule. To question the divine powers was sacrilege, to question government a form of treason. The age we are in is one where everything is questioned. It is a questioning age, and everything is undergoing such rapid change that it is well-nigh impossible to predict what life on earth will be like a hundred years from now, let alone fifteen hundred years. Life swung into the fifth epoch with great impetus. There was the advent of Renaissance Christian art; the birth of a new age of poetry and drama; the exploration of the seas and the discovery of a new world, not only North and South America, but South Africa, and later Australia and New Zealand—life on earth had suddenly expanded. Then there was also the Reformation, not in one but in many places, and the new art of printing which made the Bible available in the vernacular—that, too, was a great expansion of its own kind. But if we are to characterize the age quite particularly, our thoughts return to Galileo, the founder of the age of science. He stood much alone in his lifetime and ended his days in strict confinement under the orders of the Church. To him we ascribe three main innovations. We can do little more than name them. First, he established the law of gravitation from his study of falling bodies, later developed further by Newton. As a consequence, the laws of inertia, of the motion of lifeless objects, took possession of the human mind also in regard to the heavens, driving all spiritual considerations into the background. The stars and the planets and the earth itself became dead entities.

Secondly, with the telescope he himself had made, he confirmed what even Copernicus had only surmised, that the earth was a spinning top going round the sun, and that the sun itself rotated round an axis—everything conceived mechanically.

The third and most subtle influence to be ascribed to Galileo, and the one that has affected most deeply our view of ourselves and the world, lies in his division of human experience into two distinct categories, the quantitative and the qualitative. He was the first to formulate this, though it was adopted by Newton (who was born the day Galileo died), and by the world of science generally, down to today. Expressed in his own terms, in regard to 'a piece of matter or corporeal substance' he felt as *real* the fact that 'in its own nature it is bounded and figured in such and such a form, that in relation to others it is large or small, that it is in this or that place, in this or that time, that it is in motion or remains at rest, that it touches or does not touch another body, that it is single, few or many'. These are the qualities he sees as real and properties of the object in question. On the other hand, whether the same 'piece of matter or corporeal substance' is deemed 'white or red, bitter or sweet, sounding or mute, of a pleasant or unpleasant odour'—such qualities for Galileo only 'seem to exist'. They do not actually pertain to the object 'but hold their residence solely in the sensible body; so that if the animal were removed, every such quality would be abolished and annihilated'. This is an astonishing phenomenon, the more so for having captured the mind and imprisoned us in a certain sense. Henceforth only phenomena that submit to numerical treatment, such as weight, measure, number, motion, in other words only quantitative values are to be regarded as objectively valid for scientific investigation. All other values that engage the sensations, feelings or any other response of an inward character, the qualitative aspect of experience, is declared subjective and of no validity in determining the nature of the world. In this way the whole life of inner experience relating to art, religion, moral idealism, and indeed the human being himself and his humanity is set to one side. The human soul is split in two. As one twentieth-century thinker, Alexis Carrell, expressed it half a century ago, it is this view that had led to the triumph of technology and the degradation of man.

It is not that Galileo in his own life adhered only to his view of the physical world. All the evidence shows him to have remained at all times a devotee of the Catholic Church despite the way it treated him, for it condemned his work and held him under conditions of solitary confinement, admitting visitors only under sanction. Such a visitor, when Galileo was already old and blind and working on his magnum opus in physics, was the young poet Milton. Galileo could still live

naively and contentedly in two worlds, the physical world of
the senses as he saw it, and the religious world of faith. He
could not have foreseen that he had set in train something
that was to lead to scepticism, agnosticism, atheism and
eventually to scientific materialism, and that the prelates who
opposed him had an uneasy premonition of where his science
was to lead.

We have enlarged on this third innovation of Galileo
because it so plainly concerns the present day.

The physics which the genius of Galileo engendered has led
to universal reliance on the quantitative, making the qualitative secondary and ephemeral. Physics has affected biology,
and that it turn psychology, reducing the human being to a
phantom of himself.

This gave rise to the split between the humanities and the
sciences. After all, Shakespeare was born in the same year as
Galileo, in 1564. He took as his sphere of activity the very one
that science left out of account, the sphere of all that is
intrinsically human. There has been a great company of
poets, artists and thinkers who have sought to construct their
own world where measurement cannot apply—a world which
is very real in terms of experience. Even Galileo, himself, was
a good musician as well as a scientist, showing that we remain
human whatever our theories. But the morality and faith of
the past no longer had any ground to stand on.

The other outstanding feature of the past five centuries is
that of emancipation from authority of any kind in a search
for personal freedom. First, with the Reformation, came the
demand for freedom of belief. Then came the revolt against
monarchical rule, in France the great Revolution, in England
the civil war between the Royalists and the Roundheads
ending with the beheading of Charles I, regarded still by
many as a martyr. The idea of democracy was born. King-

ship, as constitutional monarchy, where it lingers on, has the virtue of standing aloof from governance and political parties.

And now, in this century particularly, the struggle has been and still is to find a new basis for economic life.

With priest, ruler and merchant in their earlier forms laid aside, what is left of the ancient castes but the Sudra, the fourth and humblest. We are in a real sense Sudras seen in the light of the threefold commonwealth: each has to be priest to himself or choose his own priest in freedom; each ideally has his part as ruler in the democratic life of rights; each has his responsibility, according to his gifts, to the economic life. What then is the task of the Sudra? Who is the Sudra but the individual ego? Seen this way, the whole trend is towards a threefold commonwealth.

A parapsychologist once asked me what evidence I could offer of real human progress. The only answer I could give was that in the past responsibility rested on the few whereas today it rests on each and all.

To ignore this results inevitably in states of unfreedom. This brings us back to asking what constitutes freedom, and what do human beings really live by? It is clear that the crises which meet us are reflections of the crisis in ourselves. There never can be or will be outer freedom until people have found the ground of inner freedom. Sometimes the truth of this appears in very unexpected ways.

The experiences of some of the Russian dissidents show how, under conditions of extreme physical and mental torture, inner resistance determined by an indefinable faith not to give way has allowed miracles to occur. A point can be reached where such a person is filled with an unassailable peace, with compassion even for the persecutors as being the weaker, with forgiveness and the absolute certainty that in the end things were ordained and life determined, whatever the outer pressures, by mysterious powers from within. There was a source within which remained unassailable.

Extending this more widely to the world of today, one might say: never has humanity been so wildly distracted, never so beset with mental, moral, physical threats and dangers, nor exposed to such widespread division and distrust. Never has the individual felt so abandoned in his loneliness, never so tempted to see himself as a non-entity, yet never has he been so aware that he is indeed a *self* and that it is on this discovery that the future of the world depends. Never has he heard so clearly the call from within: 'Man know thyself.' It is this awakening call that, despite all the negatives, is spreading through the world to declare in this age of contradictions what the human being truly is. It is the character of the age that has brought anthroposophy into our time, not to revive old faiths, but to bring a new knowledge of the human being to inspire new faith.

Man has lost the world of the spirit in order that he may in all freedom find the spirit in himself and, finding the spirit in himself, discover the spirit in the world anew, but now as a fully conscious member of the whole.

Thus far has our search for the meaning of history brought us. We still have to find the underlying impetus that carries us forward.

# 6
# A TIME OF TESTING

## *The child as guide*

We find ourselves endowed with a certain type of consciousness, though not one we are born with. Our children
show us this. They make us aware how hard it is to enter the
mind of childhood. The younger the child the more difficult it
is. We can hold reasonable converse with our adolescents,
partly because we still recollect something of our own youth
and how differently we then reacted to life. In the eyes of
youth we often appear as failures. They see all too clearly how
little we are able to cope with life. Deep in their feelings there
still lives a faith that can move mountains—not as they see us
move them with dynamite or other explosives. That leaves
them impressed in a way but unmoved. They carry an inner
knowledge that the world should be better than it is. In the
depths of their being, they are seekers for truth. They want to
discover and are glad to be helped to discover that there are
real goals in life and that the world is built on truth. Yet
where is this truth to be found? How are they to recognize it?
Truth must be truth. They are not fond of compromise. The
feeling for what lives beyond the rational is what they really
live by, and without this there can be no art and no religion
and in the end nothing to live for. There are truths in life,
those that touch us most deeply, that can be grasped only by
an act of imagination—what might be described as a
dreaming coming from a higher source. That is what people
still possessed naturally in the fourth post-Atlantean epoch.
And that is what we adults as a rule no longer possess. When

we say 'I' to ourselves nowadays, we feel secure in our physical body—the brain is also body. That was not so for the Ancient Greek. He still felt himself one with all nature. Rudolf Steiner tells us, for example, that the Greek sculptor had no need of a model. He still sensed the plastic formative or etheric forces that had shaped his own body and he could work out of these. He felt them objectively, therefore in early Greece art was not yet personalized. Jove, Apollo, Homer, Socrates, they bore the same likenesses no matter who the sculptors were. This is quite different in Christian art where each artist offers his own interpretation. The Greek, for example, could still experience the essential nature of the four elements: fire was hot and dry, air was warm and wet, water was cold and wet, earth was cold and dry. By these qualities he could judge the regions of the earth; he could also judge people in their dispositions and temperaments. The elemental nature spirits still lived vividly in folk imagination. They had their allotted places and their tasks. They lived not only in Greece but in many places at this period. The gnomes could hammer sunlight into gold (the dwarf Regan in the Norse myth for example), moonlight into silver, they invisibly shaped and fashioned crystal forms, but they were also busy where the plant was rooted in the earth. The undines of the watery element were to be met in the sparkling streams and brooks and mountain waterways but also in the sap of stem and leaf. The airy sylphs, said Rudolf Steiner, taught the birds their songs, but they also brought colour into the world in the opening bud and the crowning flower. And the flashing, sparkling salamanders rejoiced in flickering flames but also shot their secret fire into the forming seeds to give them power of expansion when the next sun season came. The great Italian sculptor Benvenuto Cellini tells in his autobiography how as a child he saw an elemental fire spirit, a salamander and how he ran to tell his father and how his father gave him a sound thrashing to knock such nonsense out of his head. No wonder that children have got so shy of telling things. How cold our view of nature would have been to those ancients.

To the Greeks, to see Pallas Athene or Apollo or some other god appear upon the stage was natural, but the human actors were disguised behind masks and wore high-heeled shoes to give them added stature—as humans they were not yet fully descended to the earth, not yet personalities born. The heroes stood midway between gods and humans, off-spring of a divine being and a mortal.

How then, at that time, did they experience the 'I'? When Socrates needed to solve a problem he retired to a lonely spot—he could stand for hours in deepest contemplation, communing with his *daemon*, with his higher self. What was this higher self other than his immortal nature, his ego, not yet fully incarnated. If this were understood, we would know better how to listen to our adolescents today, for though present conditions of incarnation are different and the environment too is different, yet at their stage of life they are still Greek in soul—they are not yet fully earth-born for the dream force from pre-birth is still active within them. Whether they act for good or ill largely depends on what meets them in the adult world; they still live as in dream, therefore not yet wholly responsible. They teach us that without the faculty of Imagination life is barren. If we wish to enter truly into the Greek world, the adolescent tells us we must develop Imagination, not fancifulness but what we might call a perceptive faculty that carries further than the obvious.

And now, if we are to go back to pre-adolescence, to childhood proper, how are we to convey our meaning to a 12-year-old, a 9-year-old, a 6-year-old? There is only one way; we have to become poets like the bards of old to sing heroic tales to their listening ears, for then they *will* listen. This is no exaggeration. They want to listen to us from inside, to hear the word within the word, the true Word as it echoes back from within themselves from their life before birth. What gives birth to our speech? What strives to come to utterance through us? Nothing for the young child has yet become commonplace and ordinary; if it has, then as children they become premature adults. We need to draw on the magic of the legend, the fable, the story, the more than real. At their stage all life is a parable—we offer the picture and the meaning will dawn for them in time. Truth for them is not yet in the idea but in the language of the picture. We need to know that children in these years live by the force of Inspiration. That is their mode of experiencing, though they themselves could never say it. Inspiration is related to the ear as Imagination is to the eye. Happy is the teacher who can really reach the child through the power of the word. From this, love springs naturally. The Magi *saw* the star, and that is how our adolescents need to see. The shepherds *heard* the words and that is how our children need to *hear*—the word which gives assurance 'to men of good will' of a world built on peace and harmony, and the beauty this gives rise to.

And now, looking back in history, how did the people of the third epoch, the Egyptian people of that time live? By seeing, yes, but essentially by hearing, by listening to the word of authority which guided them in shaping their lives: they heard the word of Pharaoh, and he heard the word of his counsellors, the initiate priests, and they heard what the gods had to tell. After death they listened to the words of Osiris as he summed up their previous lives and revealed the future. The ear is a more ancient and intimate organ than the eye.

Going back to the second post-Atlantean culture epoch

and to Zarathustra, all is dialogue, is direct utterance of the sun god Ahura Mazda in answer to the questioning voice of Zarathustra; and what he heard he conveyed as instruction to his listening people, to shape their lives accordingly. He was the one great mediator between the folk and their God, and the power of the word was even more immediate. It is through the word that we can cultivate the faculty of Inspiration, which has its source in a life of dialogue before birth.

It is difficult for us to understand the Middle Ages, then Greece, Egypt and Persia, with our intellectual, analytical minds of today. It is the child in these middle years and earlier who by his response or unresponsiveness can guide us. One can hear without listening but one cannot listen without hearing.

And now, going back still further to the first post-Atlantean culture epoch, to Ancient India, the priests conveyed their teachings out of the higher realms to which they had access. The Seven Holy Rishis reached heights from which the words they offered worked as magical powers, as the will of God. This they conveyed to the people. 'Thy will be done.' So it is with children in their infant years—it is not the words as words that reach them but what lives as disposition of heart and will in our words—it is this that teaches them, and what lives as moral force in our actions. It is this, not the mere outer gesture, that they imitate and by doing so become one with us. Imitation for the little child is not just copying. They live by the force of Intuition which is beyond the picture and the word, beyond Imagination and Inspiration. It is here that we reach the meaning of 'except ye become as little children, ye cannot enter the kingdom of heaven'. There is utmost tenderness but also profoundest depth in such a saying.

Further back in time, the child is still in heaven, prepar-

ing to descend to earth. In this way the child's understanding can guide us—the younger the child, the higher
must we mount in spirit to reach him. And the further we
go back in the history and prehistory of mankind, there
too, the earlier the stage the higher must we ascend in consciousness to grasp the people of those times. We should
not speak of primitive peoples but of *earlier* peoples. And
when we go back into early Lemurian times, it is as with
the child before birth, humanity has not yet descended to
earth but is biding the time for its birth. It is cross foolish-
ness to think that the modern human being has arisen out
of previous states of barbarism and savagery. If such have
been found they are merely evidence of degeneracy from
conditions where law and custom under divine and human
guidance once prevailed.

## Christ and the human ego

Biologically, despite all the differences that exist and have
existed between the peoples of the earth, humanity is one.
Whereas all the animal types divide into species, the mammal into eighty thousand, the insects into over a million,
even the primates divide, humanity remains one species. It
follows then that all the changes of consciousness we have
been describing are progressive changes in the whole of
humanity. What is this unity based on, despite all human
diversity? Even as the human ego penetrates all parts of the
human organism and makes of all that diversity of organs,
tissues and functions an all-embracing unity, we can seek a
corresponding unifying source of all nations and races.

St Paul's contention was that Christ had come for all
human beings, not for one particular people as some supposed:

Now there are diversities of gifts, but the same Spirit.

And there are differences of administration, but the same Lord.

And there are diversities of operations, but it is the same God which worketh all in all.

But the manifestation of the Spirit is given to every man to profit withal.

For as the body is one, and hath many members and all the members of that one body, being many, are one body: so also is Christ.

For by one Spirit are we all baptized into one body, whether we be Jews or Gentiles, whether we be bond or free; and have been all made to drink into one Spirit.

I CORINTHIANS 12:4

What Paul is saying is that all the different peoples with their different gifts and capacities are individual members of the one humanity imbued with one spirit, with one uniting ego. Inspired by his experience at Damascus he proclaims that that one spirit belonging to all is Christ, the Messiah for all mankind.

The Christ Paul speaks of is beyond all separate religions and Churches (by whatever name they may be called), and beyond all division into sects and categories. The One includes all without denying the particularity of each. Likewise, anthroposophy's teaching is for all without distinction.

When I first encountered anthroposophy and began to read the basic books, *Knowledge of Higher Worlds, Theosophy*, and others, I wondered why there was no mention of Christ. Even in *Occult Science* we meet the name first in connection with the Atlantean Mysteries. Later I came to see that just as Rudolf Steiner's many lectures on the Gospels were given out of the experiences he had had before he had ever read them, so he offered a wide range of spiritual studies and, indeed, a whole new cosmology in order to help us approach afresh what is the very core of anthroposophy as Christianity, freed from traditions and any form of partisanship.

In this way history, too, acquires its real meaning. By degrees we learn to understand that the Word, the Logos, the being who came to be known as Christ, has been the guiding spirit of human evolution from all times, and that Christianity, therefore, has room in it for all religions.

From spiritual heights, he has accompanied the human being in his descent into matter, reaching him and upholding him through the Mystery Schools of all the ages where he is known as the ruling spirit of the sun. He is the Light, the Life, the spirit of Love as these stream through all existence. We recall that it was the great initiate of the Sun Oracle in Atlantis who led his disciples eastward and there, in western Asia, created a spiritual centre from which guidance was given for all the successive cultural epochs we have described. The Christ was united with all of them. In Ancient India he manifested as Vishnu who ever and again sent Krishna down to intervene in times of crisis. Krishna in his teachings calls on the human being to grow more conscious as a self. He thus prepares the way for the one who will be the bringer of the I AM. In Ancient Persia he manifests as Ahura Mazda, directing man through Zarathustra to take stronger hold of earth existence and himself. In Egypt, Osiris the sun god, through his death and his restoration to the spiritual worlds, prepares human souls for the greatest of all events to come, the descent of Christ himself. To Moses he appears as the burning bush. In answer to the question, 'Who shall I say sent me,' came the words, 'Say the I AM sent you.' In Greece Apollo reflects the inner nature of the sun even as Helios reflects its outer nature so that the inner spiritual and the outer physical, like everything else typifying Greek culture, are held in balance. In this whole history Buddha, in his last incarnation as a Bodhisattva, living about five hundred years before Christ, had a great world mission to fulfil. He was the teacher of compassion not only for all human beings but for all life on this earth. By 'eliminating' the caste system from his teaching he places the onus simply on each individual and this, in itself, prepares for the free and independent position of the individual based on the experience of the I AM. Alexander in his journeys and in founding centres for renewing spiritual culture prepares the way for the universal impulse of Christ. And then comes the announcement by John the Baptist, 'The kingdom of Heaven is at hand.' Christ repeats this. Later Christ says, 'My kingdom is not of this world.' Rudolf Steiner interprets the kingdom as the I AM which Christ brings to mankind, leading us as children of God to being brothers in Christ. It was at the time when the Mysteries were most shrouded that Christ incarnated, bringing the revelation of himself into outer perceptible form.

He was in the world, and the world was made by him, and the world knew him not.
He came unto his own, and his own received him not.

And then the words:

But as many as received him, to them gave he power to become sons of God, even to them that believe in his name:
Which were born, not of blood, nor of the will of the flesh, nor of the will of man, but of God.

Who then are to be the sons of God? They who are able to receive into themselves the newborn power of the I AM, and who thus henceforth can grow to the Godhead now within them—they who in future, through Christ's deed in becoming man, will, through the endowment of the I AM, draw the creative powers of renewing light and life and love for the world from within themselves. It is thus we can interpret the words of Paul 'Not I but Christ in me'—not what the world has made of me, but what I, having received the I AM, must now make of myself and the world. Whereas before the coming of Christ human beings sought for the self in higher worlds, since the coming of Christ each one, looking into himself, can truly say with him: the I AM that I find in myself is not of this world but my task is here. Through Christ becoming man, every human being today should be able to incarnate more completely, should be more truly human on earth than ever he was before. How is it that human understanding of the Mystery of Golgotha, the death and the resurrection, has, as we have seen, grown dimmer, and that human beings, instead of finding themselves immortal in nature and fulfilling a high destiny on their planet earth, have lost the meaning of destiny and indeed of their own existence? It is this we have to explore more fully. The broad historical overview was given in the section on Kali-yuga but now we must turn to the actual influences at work. On the other hand, it is in surmounting the trials and obstacles which we are obliged to meet that we can hope to grow to our full estate.

## The adversaries

One cannot go far into spiritual science without coming to realize that adverse spiritual powers, powers of hindrance and opposition, do actually exist and are active. It is their will to deflect humanity from its rightful course of development and thus to defeat the mission of Christ.

Christopher Marlowe, born in 1564, the same year as

Shakespeare and Galileo, wrote a play, *Doctor Faustus,* on this very theme. Goethe knew the play and admired it. His *Faust* has a very similar opening.

Faustus is an accomplished scholar in several fields— Aristotelian logic, philosophy, medicine, and even theology. He is a frustrated figure, for with all his accomplishments he is no more than an ordinary man. Learning can take him no further and so he turns to necromancy, and ignoring all warnings begins to practise magic.

Mephistopheles appears, the father of lies, and inveigles Faustus into signing a contract with his own blood for a period of twenty-four years. During this time Mephistopheles will hold himself at the bidding of Faustus in all things. His blood congeals. But Mephistopheles fetches 'a chafer of coles' to dissolve it back. The blood rises against the deed, forms the words *Homo fuge*—his own blood bids him flee but he ignores it.

Faustus becomes a court magician, he can perform amazing engineering feats, can invent a flying ship to India to fetch grapes for the Duchess in the midst of winter. He brings about a wonder. With Mephistopheles at his side he calls up the shape of Helen—

Was this the face that launcht a thousand shippes
And burnt the toplesse Towres of Ilium?

All this he can do, but he wants more. He wants to penetrate to the Mysteries, to know what rules in the stars, what is heaven, what hell, but finds that Mephistopheles can only mouth the barren nothings he is all too familiar with already. He sees now he has been deceived. Curses will not help. He falls into a state of deepest gloom. Mephistopheles, alarmed lest he break his contract, fetches Lucifer, who comes leading in his trail all the seven vices to drown the soul of Faust and glut his appetites. This fails, too, for it offers him no answers.

The play proceeds. The final hour has come. The clock has struck eleven. Time moves on.

> The devil will come, and Faustus must be damnd.
> O Ile leap up to my God: who pulles me down?
> See see where Christ's blood streams in the firmament
> One drop would save my soule, halfe a drop, ah my Christ!

It does not take much to see that Marlowe was a modern spirit, ultra-modern in his time. The sheriffs were on their way to arrest him as an atheist! He was killed in a tavern brawl.

What astonishes is that Marlowe sees Christ's deed as not for the earth only but that it reaches to the far universe.

Marlowe was modern in another sense too. He broke the fetters of the old rhymed couplet and bequeathed on the English language his 'mighty line' of blank verse which Shakespeare carried to such magnificent heights—the line on which the greatest in English poetry was to be built.

We have in him one who stood at the threshold of this modern age and saw with amazing fore-vision the dangers that lay ahead—and at the same time still had knowledge of the two great adversaries, Mephistopheles and Lucifer.

Lucifer and Mephistopheles-Ahriman have been known through the ages in their different guises: Lucifer as a red-headed, dancing mischievous devil; Ahriman, dark, sinister, threatening, satanic; Lucifer as tempter of the soul; Ahriman as the deceiver, the falsifier of the spirit; Lucifer as pride; Ahriman as greed. Both appear in a host of folk-legends. But both are also known in the Mystery Schools, now one taking prominence, now the other. In Ancient India it was Lucifer taking the lead, in Ancient Persia, Ahriman; Lucifer in his mystical flight from the earth veers more towards the East;

Ahriman spelling out earthly and materialistic Utopias, leans more to the West. Lucifer and Ahriman, once we know them, are found active everywhere. It is wholly understandable, therefore, that the first experience of Christ after his descent into the sheaths of Jesus at the baptism was his encounter with them in the scene of the 'wilderness' which Rudolf Steiner translates as 'loneliness'. This scene is described almost identically in Matthew and Luke, is only hinted at in Mark with mention of 'wild beasts', and does not appear in John.

In Matthew 4:1–11 it reads as follows:

Then was Jesus led up of the Spirit into the wilderness to be tempted of the devil.

And when he had fasted forty days and forty nights, he was afterward an hungred.

And when the tempter came to him, he said, If thou be the Son of God, command that these stones be made bread.

But he answered and said, It is written, Man shall not live by bread alone, but by every word that proceedeth out of the mouth of God.

Then the devil taketh him up into the holy city, and setteth him on a pinnacle of the temple,

And saith unto him, If thou be the Son of God, cast thyself down: for it is written, He shall give his angels charge concerning thee: and in their hands they shall bear thee up, lest at any time thou dash thy foot against a stone.

Jesus said unto him, It is written again, Thou shalt not tempt the Lord thy God.

Again, the devil taketh him up into an exceeding high mountain, and sheweth him all the kingdoms of the world, and the glory of them;

And saith unto him, All these things will I give thee, if thou wilt fall down and worship me.

Then said Jesus unto him, Get thee hence, Satan: for it is written, Thou shalt worship the Lord thy God, and him only shalt thou serve.

Then the devil leaveth him, and behold angels came and ministered unto him.

In both Gospels the temptation of the turning of the stones into bread comes first. In Luke the order of the other two is reversed.

Rudolf Steiner sees working in this scene both Lucifer and Ahriman.

He places first the scene of the 'exceeding high mountain' and ascribes this to Lucifer 'who draws near to human beings when they prize the self too highly and are lacking in humility and self-knowledge'. His aim is to play on self-pride and self-glorification.

The second temptation, that of the high pinnacle, he ascribes jointly to Lucifer and Ahriman. 'Lucifer sought to goad his pride, Ahriman, to play upon his fear.' Since their ambitions are opposite they annulled each other.

In regard to the third test, that of turning stones into bread, there Ahriman acts alone. Christ, never having lived on earth, could not have known how human beings change stones, mineral substance, that is, money into bread. Ahriman uses this to his advantage. Christ, who could say, 'I am the bread of life,' is later betrayed for thirty pieces of silver.

Christ overcame Lucifer by entering into human blood and purging it of every taint of egotism. Hence, in the legend of the Holy Grail, this blood, gathered by Joseph of Arimathaea as it flowed from the side of Christ into the cup of the Last Supper, brings healing and the power of transubstantiation to the soul. Ahriman he defeats by overcoming death through the resurrection. It is left to us to unite ourselves with the deeds of Christ in freedom. Until his descent to the earth Christ guided humanity from outside as a God. Now by receiving through Christ the Kingdom of Heaven that is not of this earth, the I AM, we can rise from being children of God to brothers in Christ, thus drawing strength from within, as is meant by the words of Paul, 'Not I but Christ in me.'

## *The consciousness soul age*

The consciousness soul age is the age we are in. It is still very young. By our reckoning it is less than six hundred years old and still has over a millennium and a half to go. What this age really is or what it is intended to become will only be realized at the end of that time. All we can do is to characterize what we know of it up to the present. Our survey of childhood from the adolescent backwards was intended to help us recognize through what states of consciousness humanity has passed up to the present time; but the adolescent, not yet having arrived at adulthood, could not tell us where we are now. That is left to us to discover; and the age still being so young, we ourselves are little more than adolescent.

Let us then review what we know. We know that Galileo is the father of modern physics. He divided experience into two categories: what pertained to himself, which came to be classed as subjective, and what, in his view, pertained to the world around him and which came to be regarded as objective. All he could rely on in his objective view of the world was what he could determine by measurement. His view of the world in terms of weight, measure, number, motion has been adopted and developed to give us the science of technology as we know it. Today machines probe planetary space for many millions of miles and are accurately controlled from the earth. At the same time this earth is being subjected to pollution of its soil, water and air; and it has become the receptacle for deadly poisonous fallout of wastes that have to be buried in special containers, for the earth itself cannot cope with it. This is one glimpse of the consciousness soul age and it indicates something totally new in the history of the world.

Contemporary with Galileo was Descartes, considered the father of modern philosophy. He set out to determine what he knew that was not derived from other sources but was really his own. This cost him years of tireless research into the contents of his own mind, and led him to a remarkable conclusion. Socrates took as his starting point: 'I know that I know nothing.' Descartes came to the conclusion: 'I doubt.' But how could he doubt if he did not think? This question led him to the further conclusion: 'I doubt therefore I think.' But then, how could he think if he were not there to think, hence his further step: 'I doubt therefore I think therefore I am.' In philosophical terms he had to confirm his own existence in this circuitous manner beginning with doubt. Unfortunately this has been generally abbreviated to 'I think therefore I am'. But actually all other considerations are based on the initial circumstance of doubt. This element of doubt has spread through the world so that humanity today is plunged into doubts of every kind. Most powerfully working to disrupt life is doubt of one another. We have reached a stage where, whether at government levels or in private life, doubt affects everything. Rudolf Steiner questions the validity of the conclusion 'I think therefore I am'. He poses the question, 'Do I cease to exist when I do not think, for example, when I am asleep?' and reverses the statement to 'I am therefore I think'. That leaves open the question of where I am, in what realm and in what state of consciousness I am when asleep. Is it possible to enter consciously into the life of sleep? Is it possible to bring the life of sleep into the waking day?

Many questions and possibilities arise in this way which can be pursued actively. The alternative is the one followed by the behaviourists, deriving the conscious faculties from bodily processes alone and leading to the conclusion that 'the autonomous human being' is a fiction, that the whole idea that I am something in myself is an illusion. Even if not everybody subscribes to this conclusion, we live in a world where the individual is easily and frequently brushed aside and the human being is treated as a thing, even as a doubtful commodity. Descartes and some of his contemporaries came to the view that the animal was no more than a kind of machine. They practised vivisection and persuaded themselves that the agonized cries of the animals could be compared to the creaking of a machine. There is factual evidence that this really happened.

That people could arrive at such a view is a new development and has to be regarded as a product of the consciousness soul age.

Let us turn our attention to a different kind of evidence of our modern time. Shakespeare's Hamlet has been regarded as representative of the consciousness soul. We can dwell on a few points only.

Hamlet loved his father, loved his mother, loved Ophelia.

His 'prophetic heart' tells him that something is amiss in regard to his father's death. The Ghost, already seen by others, merely confirms what in his heart he knew already. The treachery of a brother's perfidy stands clearly before him. This question of the blood turned treacherous is a theme that Shakespeare returns to many times. This in itself shows that the world once built on the loyalty of the blood is no more, and it raises the question: what is to take its place? Then his vision of his mother, in so quickly abandoning the love and loyalty to his father to join the uncle—that vision and the trust he had in her is shattered. 'Frailty, thy name is woman.' This judgement then he turns upon Ophelia. Why does she return his gifts? What connivance may have brought that about? He does not trust her father, Polonius, but how can he trust her? His doubting head rejects her, though his heart yearns for her. Only at the end, jumping into her open grave, he declares for the whole world to hear,

I loved Ophelia; forty thousand brothers
Could not, with all their quantity of love,
Make up my sum.

So in Hamlet we see how head and heart are wrenched apart, head doubts heart and heart doubts head. Our thoughts and feelings no longer go together and so action and will are also defeated.

Hamlet could so easily have ended his life with 'a bare bodkin' but the thought of what there might be beyond death 'puzzles the will' and resolute action is paralysed by 'the pale cast of thought'.

How widely, today, is this same puzzlement felt. Again he could so easily have killed his perfidious uncle—revenge in the old style could not satisfy his soul. It could not restore the world that has been lost.

What is left him but to use the word as a sword. His biggest deed in the play is his attempt to waken the conscience of his mother—

O Hamlet, speak no more;
Thou turn'st mine eyes into my very soul,

and again,

O, speak to me no more;
These words like daggers enter in mine ears;

But then, the Ghost intervenes:

Oh, step between her and her fighting soul;

What manner of ghost is this? Can a ghost have compassion for the living and, moreover, for one who, in the eyes of Hamlet, has wronged him?

Compare the Hamlet situation to that of Orestes or any other of the great Greek tragedies and we realize that in this modern age we have entered into a totally new relationship with life, a new situation in relation to the human soul. An earlier character, Jaques, declares, 'All the world's a stage.' The stage at the end of Hamlet is littered with the dead. The stage of the world today is littered with the dead, more and more each day; and everywhere, what are or could be potential capacities of love are mutually destructive.

And now we must turn to another view of this consciousness soul age as it meets us at this very time. A cursory view sees a world full of machinery of every kind and new devices being discovered every day, a world piling up armaments of terrible might, a world that is flooded with words, in countless daily journals, weekly magazines, numberless books, radio and television unceasing, the raucous voice of humans shouting, inciting, clamouring, and wars and threats of wars going on all the time. The world has never been so noisy.

Let us look back one hundred years and what shall we see disappear? Outer space explorations and the whole of aeronautics—not a plane to be seen in the skies—maybe as a rarity an experimental balloon; no radio, radar, television; no cinemas even, and maybe the first beginning of an automobile creeping into view. A silent world, and the torrents of words cease. No question of atomic power, of nuclear threats;

Einstein's formula did not exist as yet, though radioactivity was being explored and the electron had been discovered. Now let us look back two hundred years: electric power, steam power vanish from the scene and therefore also locomotives and steamships. The hum of industry is silenced for no steam engine had yet been invented. James Watt developed his steam pump in 1765. What is left? Nature, a stage coach on the road, a sailing ship on the water, and, alas, gunpowder still on the battlefields. Only two hundred years ago.

Now reverse the process—from the steam pump, to the steam engine and the rise of new industrial populations, to the locomotives (George Stephenson's Rocket won the prize in 1829) and steamships. Faraday was at work. Already in the thirties he was discovering the laws of electromagnetism which gave rise to the dynamo, electric light and electric power available across great distances, and the harnessing of watersheds. And then the discovery and the release of atomic energy. Modern traffic is multiplying in quantity and speed, so that today there is already concern about energy resources; coal and oil will be exhausted in the not very distant future. And not to be overlooked, the triumphs of chemistry are advancing rapidly to replace natural products with synthetic ones.

But most of all we encounter horrors that might be released at any time to bring about holocausts and devastation on an unimaginable scale—this stupendous change, where all the world is interlocked as one and yet has never been more divided. What then will the picture be in two hundred years from now? The mind reels at the thought as we see civilization of today hanging on the edge of an abyss down which it might hurtle at any moment.

This amazing spectacle of accelerating 'progress', if that is what it is to be called, must have its source in an evolutionary process, but here we need the longer view that only spiritual science can give. There are two approaches which we can best follow. The following sketch may help to elucidate one of them.

| Post-Atlantean epoch | Stage of earth development | Cosmic background |
| --- | --- | --- |
| Ancient Indian epoch | Polaria | Ancient Saturn |
| Ancient Persian epoch | Hyperborea | Ancient Sun |
| Ancient Egyptian epoch | Lemuria | Ancient Moon |
| Graeco-Roman epoch | Atlantis mid-stage of the present earth | — |
| The modern epoch | — | — |

Ancient Indian culture was a repetition in terms of human experience of what had ruled as divine creative process in Polaria—which in itself, as the first stage in present earth evolution, was a recapitulation of Ancient Saturn. Likewise, Ancient Persia echoed Hyperborea, the second stage of the earth as a recapitulation of the Ancient Sun. In the same way the Ancient Egyptian epoch related to Lemuria and the Ancient Moon. Graeco-Roman culture relates through Atlantis to the middle stage of the earth.

The fifth post-Atlantean epoch is not a recapitulation of the past in a similar way. It has no such past. It marks, in the whole of cosmic-earthly evolution, a new starting point towards a state of the world as yet unborn.

Contained in this fact is the greatest secret of the present time and its most significant feature, the break with authority, with ruling traditions and orthodoxies and the ever-repeated demands for freedom, emancipation, self-determination. However they may have been misrepresented at times, freedom and emancipation take supremacy over all other calls and demands in this consciousness soul age since the fifteenth century.

For two thousand years Aristotle was held the supreme

authority in science, then came Galileo who rejected and displaced him. The Catholic Church held unquestioned authority based on apostolic succession from the time of Peter. Then came Luther pinning up his Declaration of Independence and the Reformation had arrived. Along with this came the translation of the Bible into the vernacular, so that the Holy Word became available to all. There came political emancipation from royalty; in France with all the violence of the French Revolution, in England through the civil war between the Royalists and the Roundheads. The Royalists with their cry of the divine right of kings, the Roundheads pointing to their cropped heads as the only testimony they would abide by. There then followed, politically, the idea of democracy, ideally giving to each one his share in the government of the country. We recall the American fathers seeking freedom of worship in another land—Thanksgiving Day is still nationally celebrated. And later came the American Declaration of Independence, and then the battle for the emancipation of slaves. In this century began the emancipation of women from their age-old dependence on men. One could go on extending this list, for the struggle for freedom and self-determination continues to this day, on so many fronts.

Freedom in the past meant freedom from outer bondage and compulsion. Today it has acquired a further meaning, a finding of oneself, a birth from within. At the time of the French Revolution there were many who believed that humanity was about to enter a new age of freedom. They were soon to be disillusioned. The freedom they dreamed of was to be sought elsewhere. Coleridge was one of the many to suffer disappointment. It was this that led him to write the following words:

... on that sea-cliff's verge
Where pines, scarce travelled by the breeze above
Had made one murmur with the distant surge,
Yes, while I stood and gazed with temples bare,
And shot my being through earth, sea and air,
  Possessing all things with intensest love,
    O Liberty! my spirit felt thee there.

In these words Coleridge has uttered something that speaks for the inmost character of the consciousness soul age, freedom born of the spirit out of love for all creation. This same experience is the crowning one of Shelley's *Prometheus Unbound*—only love for the world can free Prometheus from the rock to which he is bound. This is also the triumphant chorus that ends Beethoven's ninth symphony. Freedom is in the world, it lives in us, yet remains a far-off ideal, whereas in life as we meet it, all seems confusion and contradiction. Why is this?

Here we need to turn to spiritual science again for a longer and larger historical view, to elucidate the dilemma in which we find ourselves. Longing and, as we believe, striving ardently for freedom, we find ourselves caught increasingly in conditions or threats of unfreedom.

The question arises: At what point in this whole evolution does the human being himself, as conscious ego, enter into the process to play his responsible part? It cannot be while his sheaths are being prepared, his physical body, etheric body, astral body—that can only be the work of the gods. It can only be in the course of the post-Atlantean epochs as the life of thought develops and the human being advances in self-awareness. By the end of Atlantis, evolution of the physical body has reached the point where the human being walks in an upright position, and his larynx is so far formed that he can utter speech. His brain, too, has reached a stage that makes possible the lighting up of thought, but all this as a very elementary beginning. In all regards, the human being is still utterly and completely dependent on guidance from without, that is, from high initiation sources. And now we learn that in the first post-Atlantean epoch the task of the Seven Holy Rishis was to draw down the forces for shaping and perfecting the etheric body; the caste system, as we have described it, is an expression of this. So, too, the mighty task of Zarathustra was to bring order and organization into the astral body. Only then does the human ego which has been resting in and with the gods begin its descent into the three sheaths.

As the ego works upon the sheaths, so an internalized life of soul begins for the human being. Egyptian culture is the expression of the work of the ego upon the astral body, awakening the first stage of personalized consciousness as sentient soul. Astrology, or the reading of human destiny from the stars, is one aspect of the dawning sense of selfhood. Graeco-Roman culture came about through the working of the ego-forces upon the etheric body, thus giving rise to the mind soul or intellectual soul. The birth of philosophy marked a stronger degree of internalized experience and self-identity. This continued through the Middle Ages. We have only to think of such an outstanding figure as Thomas Aquinas. Then from early in the fifteenth century the ego descended into the physical body, providing the basis for today's strongly accentuated sense of selfhood with the birth of the consciousness soul. Thus the three last cultural epochs show the progression from sentient soul through intellectual soul to consciousness soul. As we have seen also in considering Kali-yuga, this process of entering into the bodies meant, on the one hand, a heightening of the sense of individuality, and on the other, the fading away of a natural awareness of the spirit at work in nature. The Egyptians with their sentient soul still retained a live relationship to the world of the stars. The Greeks in their thinking still experienced the life-creating forces in the world. We in our age have lost all that. We have developed a world view which uses logic to interpret observation confined to the outer appearance of phenomena. But this logic which we have inherited from the Greeks has lost its inner grasp of existence and become very abstract.

It is in the Graeco-Roman epoch that Christ made his ultimate descent to the earth for, as we have also seen, he was ever the guiding divinity, the bearer and upholder of the law ruling and directing human progress. At this time Christ descended to earth, to confirm by his own deed of incarnation the establishment of ego incarnation for mankind. Amongst those who were living at that time, a time when people were not as body-bound as we are, there were some, the disciples and others, who became his followers. They perceived the divinity that enveloped and penetrated the being of Jesus, though it completely surpassed their understanding. Only by slow degrees could they awaken somewhat to the mystery of the being in whose presence they lived and moved. What Christ achieved through his incarnation will eventually lead to the spiritualization and the passing away of the world through the mediation of evolving humanity. In that mystery we still live and move, for the most part unknowingly.

Under ordinary conditions today, the ego is so deeply incarnated into the physical body that, in our consciousness at the boundary of the senses, we experience ourselves as arrested there. If we look inwards, our intellectual mind reveals nothing to us of our essential being. If we gaze through our senses outwards we find ourselves strangers to the world around us. If we attempt to draw back into ourselves, we grow lost to the world. If we identify ourselves with the outer physical world we grow lost to ourselves. Either way we seem condemned to a life of loneliness and unfulfilment. Inner and outer do not meet. Thus, in our soul we lapse into a state of desolation, emptiness, alienation. We can think of T. S. Eliot's 'hollow men'.

The condition of Marlowe's Faustus typifies much of our modern condition. Unable to solve the riddle of our own being in the world around us, we all too easily become devotees of Lucifer who would lead us off into realms of mystical fantasy; or we fall a prey to the machinations of Ahriman who, with utmost cunning, infiltrates our thinking to persuade us that the world is no more than a machine and we are a replaceable part in it.

We live in dangerous times. Whether through illusory idealism or delusory realism, we can grow divorced from the source of our own being in the Logos, in Christ, denying our own true egohood. The impulse to explore, discover and create anew proceeds from the greater ego we are so apt to forget or ignore. The impulse which launched the scientific adventure and along with it the search for freedom proceeds from the very nature of the I AM. But life today is immersed in the physical and we can be trapped in this level of existence.

Anthroposophy builds on the two faculties of observation and thinking. Thinking strengthened through inner exercise and freedom from preconceived theory in observing can lead, beyond the bounds of the physical, to an enhanced consciousness that transcends what are today regarded as the limits of knowledge, both in regard to the world outside and the life within. Then we begin to awaken also to the workings of Lucifer and Ahriman, to the part they play in the world and therefore also in us. We cannot merely flee from them but we can learn to direct to human ends the forces they exert.

Then the term consciousness soul can acquire a new name, spiritual soul. We have not yet awakened in the spirit but we have awakened to it. Life takes on a new character and human endeavour a new direction. We begin to see more clearly why we cannot live any longer by drawing wisdom from the past, necessary as this may be for the understanding of the present, but we are called on to shape a future out of the intuitive powers of the will. Here, humanity without the Christ-ened ego to help, is in great danger of losing its way between Lucifer the tempter and Ahriman the deceiver.

Consciousness soul or spiritual soul means to recognize the situation of modern man in full consciousness, to awaken to the particular dangers and temptations which this age offers, and to know what measures need to be taken to meet them, measures to be born as free initiatives.

## Reincarnation and individual destiny

The teaching of reincarnation has lived in the East from ancient times and was renewed and reformed by the Buddha in the sixth century BC. It never established a place in Christian tradition. Today we find it presented with a different emphasis in anthroposophy. Let us consider these three conditions of consciousness.

The Buddha stands as the great teacher of compassion. He saw earth existence as steeped in pain and grief. Birth is suffering, age is suffering, sickness is suffering, death is suffering; but also being separated from those we love is suffering, being compelled to live with what we do not love is suffering, being unable to fulfil one's desires is suffering. The cause of these ills he attributed to the lust, the craving for sense-bound living, which possessed the soul. The only way to overcome this was through exercising wise restraint in all respects and cultivating a meditative life. Only this could lead to the peace and tranquillity necessary for the soul to free itself from the bondage of repeated lives on earth. The Buddha, having overcome temptation and having achieved illumination, knew that never again would he himself have to live in an earthly body. Out of his own experiences he taught the Eightfold Path, whereby every soul that persevered could gain similar release and win the way to Nirvana, the land of bliss and blessedness. This striving aims to reattain the primordial virtues from which life on earth has fallen away.

The Path is expressed very simply in words and made accessible to everyone. It can be briefly expressed as follows:

Right understanding and right aspiration in contemplating life;
Right speech, right conduct, and right vocation in our daily dealings with life;
Right effort, right wakeful awareness, right concentration in transcending the hold of life.

This, in broad terms, is Dharma, the way of Truth.

The Christian emphasis has always been on life in the present—not Christ WAS, but Christ IS. 'The Kingdom of Heaven is at hand,' said John the Baptist, to which Christ added, 'My Kingdom is not of this world.' Henceforth the human being, looking into himself, may come to learn that the central core of his being, his I AM, belongs to the kingdom whence Christ descended. 'And the Word became flesh and dwelt among us.' The Word, which was from the beginning, had entered the stream of earthly human evolution. 'Heaven and earth will pass away but my word will not pass away.'

Therefore our task is in this world, the world in which all

things have been bound for our sake, in which all that has been bound is waiting to be unbound. In the words of Paul, 'All nature groaneth and travaileth waiting upon the redemption of man.' Human progress and world progress are one; the words 'I am with you always' can be understood to have been spoken for all mankind, for the living as well as the dead who, in their sphere, have their tasks also.

The determining aspect here is that everything is to happen in the ever-renewing present. It thus came about that the holiest striving in the Christian centuries was to walk in the footsteps of Christ and, in esoteric terms, to meditate on the stages of the Passion: the washing of the feet; the flagellation; the crowning with thorns; the crucifixion; the death on the cross; the resurrection and the ascension. Christ's last words at parting as given in the Acts are as follows: 'And he said unto them, It is not for you to know the times and the seasons, which the Father hath put in his own power. But you shall receive power, after that the Holy Ghost shall come upon you; and ye shall witness unto me both in Jerusalem, and in Samaria, and unto the uttermost part of the earth.'

The Word is for all humanity. Ten days later came Pentecost and the descent of the Holy Ghost, the Holy Spirit, upon the disciples as they sat gathered in an 'upper room'. They were to convey what they had received to all mankind, to each one in his own tongue, which can also mean in the measure of his understanding.

Christ brought us ever-recurring life in the present. 'I am in the Father, and ye in me, and I in you'. The words 'Even as ye have done it unto the least of my brethren, ye have done it unto me', are as true this very day as ever they were then. With the emphasis on the NOW, the teaching of reincarnation vanished from view.

'By this shall all men know that ye are my disciples, if ye have love for one another.'

We live in a mystery that is unending. Hence the closing words of the Gospel of St John of which Rudolf Steiner made special mention.

'And there are many other things that Jesus did, the which, if they should be written every one, I suppose that even the world itself could not contain the books that should be written. Amen.'

Entry into the consciousness soul epoch has brought humanity to a totally new evolutionary stage. The direction of life has now swung strongly towards the future. It is an age where will is uppermost. We have seen this in the release of steam power, electric power, and now nuclear power, rapidly transforming the face of the earth. Human beings have to come to terms with themselves as never before. We have to achieve a great moral and spiritual advance or see ourselves inwardly and outwardly overwhelmed by the powers which, almost unwittingly, we have ourselves released. This situation has assumed gravest proportions, precisely in the twentieth century, since the end of Kali-yuga. A veritable struggle is being waged between the force of the awakening spirit and the materialistic powers ranged against it.

The knowledge of reincarnation, which may come newly to us through anthroposophy, should play a considerable role in securing human balance. Born of an understanding of the human being which extends beyond the limitations of birth and death, it opens up new vistas for the future.

Let us return to the view of the human being in his three-fold nature of thinking, feeling and will. With our thinking we can survey the past. We can bring the fruits of the past to have bearing on the present. What we cannot do with our thinking is to project ourselves into an actual future—we may have surmises, hopes and expectations, but that is all. With our will the opposite is the case. We can initiate deeds in the present for fulfilment in the future. What we cannot do with our will is re-enter the past—we cannot will backwards. With our feeling we can strike a balance between the fruits of the past and intentions for the future, and thus hope to arrive at present judgement.

We can pursue these considerations further. With every emerging thought, feeling, word or deed we place the impress of our being upon the world around us. Something has parted from us to find a place in the world. This, however, works back equally upon ourselves, setting its mark in us.

Rudolf Steiner once illustrated the nature of destiny (or karma) in the image of a bow and arrow. The arrow leaves the bow with a certain force, but in the same measure produces a recoil in the bow. In life we are the bow, and our thoughts and feelings and actions are the arrows we send into the world around, but we bear the recoil in ourselves.

Let us take this a stage further. At the end of the day we retire to sleep. When we waken in the morning we are not in the same condition as the night before. Something transpires between sleeping and waking. How we have lived in the day is inscribed in us, and we meet it in the night. Sleep brings change. In the alternations of day and night something is achieved which we may observe, and life develops accordingly. Our observation and judgement during the night of the day that has passed is completely objective and this works objectively in us, enabling us to develop and grow.

This then is how individual destiny works from day to day, and is seen in its results. Whatever other powers may come to meet us in the night to renew health and strength for the morrow, by what we do, or fail to do, and by our manner of doing, we are still the prime arbiters of our own individual destinies.

We can come to see how justifiably sleep has been likened to a younger brother of death. In death we leave the world behind us with all we have impressed upon it. Inevitably we carry the counterpart of this with us through death. But what we have left behind is as much a part of us as what we bear away. The one belongs to the other, and as egos we are equally involved in both.

If day and night are absolute conditions of our daily life, so that day is unthinkable without night or night without day, the same applies to the connection between life and death. We are not born in the morning out of a state of nothingness but out of the day before; we bring with us a preparedness for the new day. So, too, we may consider that we enter the world through birth uniquely equipped in our different ways for a new life. Where could we have gathered this equipment other than through a life or many lives before. To attribute all this to an ad hoc adjustment of inherited genes may seem an easy thought, but it leaves too much out of account. A human being in his ego, or I AM, is an indivisible unity, as distinct from a personality composed of many parts.

It is our own self we meet in the world in the impress we have laid upon it. It is our own destiny we meet in those we have met before, to carry our mutual adventure further. In the vast complex of human relationships we may learn to know ourselves while being responsible to one another, each to all and all to each. Looked squarely in the face, it cannot be otherwise. Where and when and at what point we meet one another, at what ages, older or younger, ceases to be casual and takes on a depth of meaning. We make room in our lives for one another. In this new age we also make room for the gods to re-enter, so that the story of humanity and the world begins once again to assume an epic grandeur. Should there be some who say, 'But this is mere make-believe,' we can only reply, 'God bless the make-believe' since it endows our relationships with a greater, more meaningful reality. But truth needs no apologist; it proves itself. Experience adds to experience and evidence to evidence if we are attentive. Every individual advance is a gift to the whole community, every failure or shortcoming a loss to all, so closely knit are our lives together. The totality of existence will not allow anybody to be left out or cast aside.

The study of reincarnation in the form now given is not based on mere belief. It opens up a great field for study and exploration. It puts human encounters into a context of many lifetimes. That few, at the present time, recall their past lives can only be counted a blessing, for there is a risk of countless illusions unless the soul is sufficiently purified and freed from all self-love.

Many have a will to return to the earth, a will to meet one another here on earth to descend from the kingdom that is not of the earth in order to fulfil the needs of the earth, so that Christ's deeds for humanity and the world shall not have been in vain. Then the words 'Where two or three are gathered in my name, there am I also' become a seed of promise that can multiply to include in course of time the whole of humanity.

In earlier times communities nurtured by an inherited past sustained the individuals composing them. From now on and into the future, in this age of light which we have entered, individual human beings will, out of their moral independence and inner freedom, create and sustain new communities in the spirit.

The future rests on the free-born deeds of men and women who have learnt to know one another in the spirit. We are moving into a future when the vicarious deed of Christ for all mankind will become the archetype of human deeds for one another. Then we will know that Christ moves amongst us, the guiding Lord of human destiny.

It is clear that no one can offer fruit to another unless he has laboured and brought forth that fruit. A newly arising conscience in modern human beings involves labouring and bringing forth fruit for one another. May he who named himself 'I am the I am', and whom we have learned to name the Christ, be with us in our mutual labours.

# 7
## TOWARDS THE FUTURE

### *The confrontation with death*

We begin to see, with the help of anthroposophy, that the human story, far from being a mindless process of chance and probability as suggested by modern science, involves all the hierarchies known to antiquity and the early Church, reaching up to the Holy Trinity, and the adversary forces which derive from these same hierarchies. One direct consequence of that adversarial opposition is the phenomenon of death following on the Fall.

It is to be noted that Genesis has two distinct accounts of the Creation. The first one proceeds from day to day, in all tranquillity. When everything else had been prepared, then God said, 'Let us make man in our own image . . . in the image of God created he him; male and female created he them.' Then came the seventh day on which 'God ended his work', and that was the day of rest.

> And God blessed the seventh day, and sanctified it: because that in it he had rested from all his work which God created and made.

There is no hint of anything adverse, of a temptation and a fall. This whole account suggests creation from Ancient Saturn and Ancient Sun up to the end and conclusion of Ancient Moon, by which time the creation of man was already incipient, hence the second version begins with 'the generations of the heavens and the earth when they were first created'. Then very soon there is mention of the creation of man: 'And the Lord God formed man of the dust of the ground, and breathed into his nostrils the breath of life; and man became a living soul.' There follows, immediately after, the creation of the Garden of Eden ... 'the tree of life also in the midst of the garden, and the tree of knowledge of good and evil'.

Next God put the man into the garden to tend it—only plants have been mentioned so far. Then comes mention of 'the man' being alone. 'I will make him an help meet for him.' But before that happens the Lord God formed every beast of the field and every fowl of the air, and brought them to Adam, having now received his own name, to be named by him. Adam was thus raised above all the new creation up to that time, with a consciousness superior to all the beasts. Only then did God cause 'a deep sleep to fall upon Adam, and he slept'. And from the side of Adam, as an extension of his being, did he create a woman ... 'and they shall be one flesh'. It is stated that 'they were both naked, the man and his wife, and were not ashamed'. They were in a state of paradisial bliss, with a consciousness that rested wholly in God. The trees of knowledge of good and evil and of life had already been shown to Adam before the creation of Eve, with a warning not to eat of the former, 'for in the day that thou eatest thereof thou shalt surely die'; not that they were never to eat of it, but they were not yet mature enough to do so. No similar warning is given about the tree of life.

Then came the serpent 'more subtil than any beast of the field' to tempt the woman. She quoted God's warning to Adam, 'Ye shall not eat of it, neither shall ye touch it lest ye die.' Now as yet there had been no death in the world. The serpent, therefore, could have known nothing about death. He assures her that God will not have her die. 'Your eyes shall be opened, and ye shall be as gods, knowing good and evil.'

Through Lucifer they were jumped prematurely into a consciousness for which they were not ready. They were filled with apprehension and beheld each other with new eyes. They were thrust into a different condition of life. The eyes that had beheld God could no longer see. The eyes they now possessed were to lead to an outer seeing but remained blind to God.

This second story Rudolf Steiner places in Lemuria which recapitulates the Ancient Moon. As the human being, towards the end of Lemuria, was emerging into his own true shape in uprightness before God, Lucifer, previously fallen from his own high estate, came to insinuate himself into the human soul. Being of a supersensible nature, he sought to establish a domain in the supersensible nature of the human being, who was thus first brought to confusion and grief.

Henceforth the human being, in the words of Faust, carried two souls within his breast; he became a divided nature, more deeply sunk in matter than he should have been, thus blinded in soul and maimed in body, leading to death. The Bible tells that God made 'coats of skins and clothed them' and he said, 'Behold the man has become one of us to know good and evil'; but they were cast out of Eden lest Adam 'should put forth his hand and take also of the tree of life, and eat, and live for ever'. Henceforth death must be their portion; but then, also, the overcoming of death by a divine deed in compensation for the deed of an adversary god, so that separation through death might be overcome by the power of love, and freedom be born, and the mission of the earth be fulfilled as 'love in freedom'.

Christ's deed in entering the stream of human destiny, in suffering death with the human being, was to plant in us the seed of immortality, so that each one, uniting himself with the Christ deed, might find the forces ultimately to overcome Lucifer himself, and conquer the death forces that assail his soul.

We may ask why Christ did not come at the midpoint of Atlantis, which was the actual midpoint of all earth evolution. Rudolf Steiner explains that owing to the displacement of the bodies through the deed of Lucifer, Christ waited for a period as long after that midpoint as the one from the temptation to that midpoint. Hence he descended to earth during the fourth post-Atlantean epoch.

Christ, after the resurrection, was able to teach the disciples as no other God has taught before or since for he alone of all supersensible beings had suffered death. He implanted in them a seed for all future times until the passing away of the world. At the end of those forty days, on the day of the Ascension, as his parting words before he was to vanish from their view, he said that the Holy Spirit would come upon them and with the power it would bring them they were to bear witness of what they had experienced 'unto the uttermost part of the earth'.

The confrontation with Ahriman still needs to be considered. When Adam and Eve, through Lucifer, were cast out of Paradise, when the light in which they had lived in Paradise was extinguished in their souls, they found themselves in an outer world that was cold, dark and imbued with death, the domain of Ahriman. Christ had overcome him for the sake of the human being, but the battle to be waged by the human being himself still lay ahead. For that we turn to the Book of Revelation. The tremendous imaginations in this book bear the character of prophetic visions of humanity's further destiny.

'And there appeared a great wonder in heaven; a woman clothed with the sun, and the moon under her feet, and upon her head a crown of twelve stars.'

Thus a figure of cosmic dimensions.

'And she being with child cried, travailing in birth, and pained to be delivered.'

There is then described 'a great red dragon' whose 'tail drew the third part of the stars of heaven'.

The dragon stood before the woman ready 'to devour her child as soon as it was born'.

'And she brought forth a man child' who was caught up unto God, and to his throne.

Then is described a mighty war in heaven, in which Michael and his angels fought the dragon and his angels. And the dragon and his host were cast out of heaven and down upon the earth.

Who was the man-child newly born? Who but the true ego in man, the I AM—that was 'to rule all nations with a rod of iron'—iron as an image of the purified will that rules in the blood, won for man 'by the blood of the Lamb'.

But then the words follow: 'Woe to the inhabiters of the earth and of the sea! for the devil is come down unto you, having great wrath, because he knoweth that he hath but a short time.'

Thus the war that was fought and won in heaven now descends to earth to be continued amongst human beings.

We recall that Lucifer slipped into the unsuspecting soul when it was still in its earliest infancy, that even at the end of Atlantis human consciousness could be compared to a child of 3 saying 'I' for the first time. And we have followed how that selfhood awareness has strengthened from epoch to epoch. All through the fourth epoch, even, the human soul was still under protection. It is only in the present age, in the age of the consciousness and spiritual soul, that the human ego has begun really to come into its own as a conscious and independent individuality, as the 'man-child', to usher in the age of freedom. The above description in the Book of Revelation, whatever other truths it may contain, most certainly has relevance for the time we are in. We are daily engaged in a battle for the freedom of the human spirit against powers that would quell that freedom. We live in an age in which death has grown rampant. We meet it in forms that would subjugate soul and spirit, not to speak of the threats of physical annihilation. We need to know the dragon before we meet him. But we need also to know that he has been overcome in higher realms and that this is the age, if ever there was one, in which humanity is being tested to the full. Wars, greater and lesser, are breaking out everywhere, and these must continue until the spirit has prevailed in inner battles. The further act of that great drama rests on humanity. Anthroposophy has come at this much needed time to awaken, to nourish, and to fortify the human spirit.

## *This Michael Age*

Michael today is little more than a legendary figure even though there is a day in the calendar, September 29, dedicated to him. And to speak of a Michael Age is well-nigh incomprehensible to most people. Yet anthroposophy has much to say about him, the archangel who was ever closest to Christ in his service to the human being. Indeed, anthroposophy in the form in which we have received it comes as Michael's awakening call, 'Man, know thyself!,' developed by Rudolf Steiner into a spiritual language for today.

The following Celtic verse shows how strongly Michael still lived in the imagination of people not so very long ago.

> Thou Michael the Victorious,
> I make my circuit under thy shield.
> Thou Michael of the white steed
> And of the bright, brilliant blade,
> Conqueror of the dragon

> Be thou at my back.
> Thou ranger of the heavens,
> Thou warrior of the King of All,
> Thou Michael the Victorious,
> My pride and my guide,
> Thou Michael the Victorious,
> The glory of mine eye.

In former times a peasant, at the end of his day's labour in the field, gazing into the sunset, might well pray to Michael to carry him under his wings to the throne of God—so warmly did Michael live in the hearts of simple folk.

We learn from Steiner that Michael inspired Alexander the Great, the pupil of Aristotle, on his great journeys to establish centres for rekindling and renewing Mystery wisdom, otherwise dying out, in preparation for the coming of Christ.[1]

Michael, we learn, was the guiding spirit of the Arthurian Mysteries which date back in origin to several centuries before Christ. The Knights of the Round Table formed a spiritual community in the service of the Cosmic Christ, the Sun-Logos, the Sun-Hero, the King of the Elements working in nature. They could therefore be called pre-Christian Christians, though the Fellowship did continue also into the early Christian centuries.

Michael was equally the guiding spirit of the Grail Mysteries in the guardianship of the Templar Knights.

The Arthurian Fellowship broke up by disruption from within, the Grail Fellowship by destruction from without. In both instances the dragon appeared to prevail. Indeed, the battle with the dragon is a recurring one at every stage of human history where a forward step is to be taken. Then the

---

[1] *Cosmic Christianity and the Impulse of Michael.* Lecture series. Torquay 1924.

adversary powers we have described gather their fullest strength, a historic crisis ensues, and the battle is renewed. We are involved in a gathering worldwide crisis at this time and man's share in it is unprecedented.

Since we have shown that the archangel Michael is active always, what makes our times a *Michael Age*? And what is the particular form the dragon assumes at this time?

We learn from Steiner how each cultural epoch has a prevailing character under the dominion of an archai or spirit of personality. We learn further that such an epoch is divided into seven sub-periods of about three hundred and fifty years, each such sub-period in the care of a particular archangel. There are seven such archangels who take charge in rotation. During the allotted time, each of these archangels is able to unfold his special gifts within the pervading character established by the archai. Michael is such an archangel and from the year 1879 he has taken over the leadership, so that everything we can call Michaelic has an opportunity at the present time of influencing human life most profoundly. We will return to this.

And now with regard to the dragon, we see him as twofold in character, bitterly divided yet single in purpose to undermine the cosmic plan for humanity. This twofoldness is expressed in the figures of Lucifer and Ahriman. In the medieval picture of the dragon we see him belching forth fire and fury whilst outwardly ensheathed in a mail of deathly coldness—unrestrained passion and unmitigated hate. There are times when it is Lucifer who appears to predominate, in which case Mephistopheles or Ahriman acts in a secondary capacity, and at other times the reverse is the case. In Faustus we saw Mephistopheles with his cold and calculating cunning as the active agent; there comes a moment when he calls in his Lord Lucifer. Both have their parts to play. Today, and ever since the dawn of a science divorced from human values, it is clearly Ahriman who is everywhere dominant; he is now the Lord, with Lucifer acting a secondary role. The cold hate of Ahriman is a passion which seizes people and proliferates cruelty and destruction without conscience; and the wiles of Lucifer to lull the soul through all manner of self-indulgences and distractions carry a deadly sting in them. Today we see ample evidence of both.

In Raphael's painting of St George and the dragon we see in the distance the figure of a young woman kneeling in prayer and supplication that she be not devoured by the dragon. This kneeling figure represents the human soul. Very different is the picture in the Book of Revelation where Satan rises up to devour the man-child the moment it is born. The man-child is the human spirit, the I AM, whose arrival has been long prepared for and now the moment has come. Ahriman wishes to destroy conscious egohood so that no being shall arrive to rule with a rod of iron—iron as human will. His aim is to produce a race of spirit-less, will-less beings—'hollow men'.

How may we interpret the picture in the Book of Revelation in today's terms.

To answer this we have to open up an aspect of the working of the archangel Michael which, so far, only anthroposophy has been able to reveal: his relationship to the life of thought. The Celtic verse we quoted describes Michael as 'ranger of the heavens'. Anthroposophy or spiritual science describes him as the ruler of cosmic intelligence. All the heavenly bodies are directed in their motions and changing relationships by divine intelligences. It was Michael's task to coordinate this weaving, working, interrelating of multiple intelligences into an integrated whole and to convey it to mankind on earth. In the past, even after the birth of Greek philosophy, there had not yet arisen the feeling of 'I think', but rather 'a God thinks in me'. A thought was something borne towards one by an angel being or divine messenger. Such thoughts then came as divinely given.

And here comes the great mystery. Even as Christ inclined himself more and more towards mankind until he placed his being totally into human hands, so, ever faithful to Christ, Michael allowed his rulership of cosmic intelligence to pass to the human being. From about the ninth century AD people increasingly began to experience thoughts as arising from within themselves, and less and less as derived from a higher source; until, with the birth of the consciousness soul, with the immersion of the human spirit in the physical body, there awoke, as we have described it, a highly accentuated sense of selfhood but at the same time a loss of conscious connection with the spirit. The human being began to regard his thoughts not even as arising from within himself but merely as mental reflections of the physical processes around him. With his blindness to the spirit in nature, the human being, seeing himself as no more than a piece of nature, arrived at a thinking which not only denies the divine but also his own actual being. To this type of thinking, empty of God, the words of Christ 'My kingdom is not of this world' cease to have any meaning.

All this was foreseen as an unavoidable precondition for an age of freedom. But unless humanity can emerge from this trial in which the gods appear to have abandoned us to alienation from reality, the human being must inevitably multiply unfreedom to the point where he is in danger of annihilating his being altogether. This danger lay ahead.

The time was approaching for the present Michael Age. It was the time when, from Galileo on, the whole trend of thinking plunged towards scientific materialism. On earth the ruling archangel was Gabriel. In the spiritual worlds, so anthroposophy tells us, during this very time, the archangel Michael assembled a mighty school attended by discarnate human souls and hierarchical beings. There he portrayed in mighty imaginations the history of the creation and evolution of the world and the human being, the mission of Christ for man from the first beginning, the place of the adversary powers in this history and much else that later formed the content of anthroposophy. This great supersensible school reached a culmination in the nineteenth century.

In the meantime the region in the heavens closest to the earth was darkened by hosts upon hosts of what are described as 'demonic idols', the dead materialistic thoughts streaming up from the earth. This was the gathering of the hosts of darkness. And there came about a war in heaven in which Michael and those who were with him fought these demonic forces. Rudolf Steiner speaks of the fall of the spirits of darkness in the forties of the nineteenth century. They were cast out of heaven and have since been rampant on earth, achieving miraculous external achievements through human beings, yet obliterating human values and the meaning of life.

It was early in the eighteen-sixties that Marx produced a work of genius in his *Das Kapital*. However this stood life on its head by making the acquisition of material resources the starting point for human progress. In the late fifties of this century had come Darwin's famous work, *The Origin of Species*, which presents man as the outcome of chance variations, again giving matter pride of place as the starting point for evolution. Then came a variety of further developments: hypnotism which made instincts the basis of soul experience; the materialistic interpretation of the heavens with the aid of the newly discovered spectroscope—and so on. The human being, thinking himself the originator of his own thoughts, lost all conception that they might be inspired by powers inimical to his being, as Rudolf Steiner shows in his *Four Mystery Dramas*.

The war in heaven became a war on earth. Rudolf Steiner was born in 1861. The new Michael Age as described by him began in 1879. He was 19 when he first realized what his mission might be: overcoming the dragon by entering into him and transforming him from within. In practice he was to enter fully into contemporary materialistic thinking and transform it so as to make of natural science a pathway to spiritual science. If we are to speak of the dragon today, it is Mephistopheles-Ahriman-Satan we have to deal with, by whatever name we choose to call him. His attack is on the man-child, the ego-bearer, the conscious thinker in human beings in this modern age.

Rudolf Steiner describes how a ray of light from the supersensible school of Michael entered the soul of Goethe, and this gave rise to his fairy tale *The Green Snake and the Beautiful Lily* in which darkness is overcome, bonds are set free, and all ends in universal rejoicing at the coming of a New Day. He describes how he felt a strong need to meditate on this work. Twenty-one years later, he wrote the first of his four mystery plays, *The Portal of Initiation*, a transformation, or better, a metamorphosis in many respects of Goethe's fairy tale. In these mystery plays we are given examples of the path of inner development as this expresses itself in a number of very different individuals. It is a path which has to find a human way between the temptations of Lucifer and the beguilement of Ahriman. The way to spiritual science opens the way to a new understanding of the Word. Inner and outer meet at a stage of new birth in the human being, so that the consciousness soul, so deeply plunged in matter, transforms into the spiritual soul, a new awakening to the spirit.

This Michael Age has no precedent in that the initiative falls wholly upon the human being—else it could not be an age of freedom. We may say that Michael is there beside us and Christ is ever with us, but it is left to us ourselves to overcome, in our thinking, the ahrimanic materialistic thinking which would dominate us. By our own endeavours we must arrive at Michaelic truth, at a way of exploring and interpreting phenomena which transcends the abyss between self and world, and thus overcome the moral void and inner emptiness which is leading civilization into increasing chaos. This is an opportunity for us, as never before, to assert our moral identity before God and ourselves. As humanity achieves the inner Michaelic victory so Michael himself may hope to regain his office as regent of cosmic intelligence in marvellously new fashion through the human soul.

How should we work in relation to modern science? Rudolf Steiner gives an accurate description of the way he himself worked. We have quoted something similar before, but here we have his precise words:

> ...study the system of Haeckel with all its materialism; study it, and at the same time permeate yourselves with the methods of cognition suggested in *Knowledge of Higher Worlds*. Take what you learn in Haeckel's *Anthropogenesis*. In that form it may very likely repel you. Learn it nevertheless; learn all that can be learned about it by outer natural science and carry it towards the gods. You will get what is related about evolution in my *Occult Science*. Such is the connection between the feeble, shadowy knowledge which human beings can acquire here, and what the gods can give us, if with the proper spirit we duly prepare ourselves by acquiring this knowledge. But the human being

must first bring towards them (i.e. the gods) what he can learn here on the earth, for in truth the times have changed.

We carry up into a spiritual world the knowledge of nature here attained, or again, the creations of naturalistic art, or the religious sentiments working naturalistically in the soul. (Even religion has become naturalistic nowadays.) And as we carry all this upwards—if we develop the necessary faculties—we do indeed encounter Michael.

Rudolf Steiner describes how in earlier times people could meet Michael as in a kind of dream, but 'since the end of the last third of the nineteenth century, human beings can meet Michael in the spirit, in *a fully conscious way*'.

But how does Michael react to our endeavours?

Michael is a being who reveals nothing if we ourselves do not bring him something from our diligent spiritual work on earth. Michael is a silent spirit—silent and reserved. Michael is taciturn. He is a spirit who speaks very little. At most he will give sparing indications, for what we learn from Michael is not really the word, but, if I may so express it—the look, the power, the direction of his gaze.

This is because Michael concerns himself most of all with what human beings *create* out of the spirit. He lives with the consequences of all that human beings have created. The other spirits live more with the causes: Michael lives with the consequences. The other spirits kindle in us the impulse for what we do. Michael is the true spiritual hero of freedom; he lets people act, and he then takes what becomes of human deeds, receives it, and carries it on and out into the cosmos, to continue in the cosmos what human beings themselves cannot yet do with it.

For other beings of the hierarchy of the Archangeloi, we

feel that impulses are coming from them. Michael is the spirit from whom no impulses come to begin with; for his most characteristic epoch is the one now at hand when things are to arise out of human freedom. But when we do things out of spiritual activity, or inner freedom ... then Michael carries the earthly deed out into the cosmos; so it becomes cosmic deed. Michael cares for the results; the other spirits care more for the causes.

However, Michael is not only a silent, taciturn spirit. Michael meets human beings with a very clear gesture of repulsion for many conceptions which the human being of today still harbours. For example, all knowledge relating to human, animals or plant life that tends to lay stress on inherited characteristics—on all that is inherited in physical nature—is such that we feel Michael constantly repelling it, driving it away with deprecation. He means to say that such knowledge is of no help to us at all for the spiritual world. Only what we discover in the human, animal and plant kingdoms independently of purely hereditary nature can be offered up before Michael. Then we receive, not the eloquent gesture of deprecation, but the look of approval which tells us that it is a thought righteously conceived in harmony with cosmic guidance.

He also sternly rejects all separating elements such as human language. So long as we only clothe our knowledge in these languages and do not carry it right up into our thoughts, we cannot come near Michael.

Among the things that today strive to reject the impulse of Michael are divisive feelings of nationality. These flared up in the nineteenth century and became strong in the twentieth—stronger and stronger. The principle of nationality has had a hand in ordering many things, or rather badly disordering them.

All this is in terrible opposition to the Michael principle; all this contains ahrimanic forces which strive against the inpouring of the Michael force into human life on earth. So then we see this battle of the ahrimanic spirits, fighting against descending spiritual impulses, who would like to carry upwards what comes through the inherited impulses of nationality—which Michael strongly rejects and repels.

The world must receive once more the principle of initiation as one of the principles of civilization. Only this will enable the human being, here on the earth, to gather in his soul something with which he can go before Michael, so as to meet Michael's approving look, the look that says: 'that is right, cosmically right'. This strengthens and stabilizes the will, and the human being is thus incorporated in the spiritual progress of the universe. Then we ourselves collaborate in what Michael is preparing to instil into the evolution of mankind on earth—beginning now in this present epoch of Michael.

### *The Group—a testimony*

Rudolf Steiner was at one time occupied with the question of how to portray the countenance of Christ.

I was once given a volume of portraits of Christ. There were reproductions from many great artists. Each one, in his own inimitable way had captured something of the quality through what lived in his own soul. Immensely different though these renderings were, they bore witness to an ideal, a source that lived in them all—each one's testimony so far as his individuality could reach.

Was it possible to go further, to conceive of a countenance that was beyond the personal and yet universally human? Was not that the striving of every great artist—to surpass the personal for the universally human? Rudolf Steiner's approach to the question was remarkably unexpected. Briefly it was as follows.

The human being is contained in a body which separates him from everything around him. This is a fact of his destiny. Through this condition of separation he knows himself to be distinct from everything else in the world. This condition of separation provides for three fundamental qualities of experience: wonder, compassion and conscience.

Only through our separation can we awaken wonder at the world in all its manifestations. The soul is moved to feelings of wonder. The Greeks said: 'Philosophy begins with wonder.' There is no comprehension of the world without the sense of wonder which carries us beyond mere seeing. How sad and impoverished is the soul that is lacking in wonder.

Compassion also we can only awaken and develop through the fact of separation. Compassion means literally 'to suffer with', to enter into the sorrows and needs of another. How desolate to have no compassion in one's heart for others. We may think of the Buddha and how all his teaching was born out of his compassion.

And then conscience. We have seen how conscience awoke in the *Orestes* of Euripides. Orestes was made to confront a wrong and his conscience gave him no peace, for the wrong demanded to be righted.

Before the birth of conscience people lived by the law that set the will of God before them. How did Christ deal with this?

And the scribes and Pharisees brought unto him a woman taken in adultery; and when they had set her in the midst, they said unto him, master, this woman was taken in adultery, in the very act. Now Moses in the law commanded us that such should be stoned: but what sayest thou?

Jesus stooped down and wrote something into the body of the earth, the earth which is the bearer of human destiny and of which he was to say, 'This is my body.' He had also said, 'I am come to fulfil the law,' that is, to bring the law as it has been till now to a conclusion. He continued to write, 'as though he heard them not'. But when they importuned him further for an answer he rose and said, 'He that is without sin among you, let him first cast a stone at her.' He continued to write into the earth—was it to inscribe into her history the arrival of the new law? 'And they, which heard it, being convicted by their own conscience, went out one by one, beginning at the eldest...' Jesus looking up found the woman alone, and asked her where were her accusers, 'hath no man condemned thee?' 'She said, No man, Lord. And Jesus said unto her, Neither do I condemn thee: go, and sin no more.'

We should note that there is no question here of remission of sins as commonly interpreted. Each one still has to awaken his conscience to deal with his own sin, otherwise there would be no room for freedom. Christ took upon himself the redemption of the earth from the cosmic sin of Lucifer. And even if people atone for their own sins, each sin committed does injury to the earth: it is this that Christ took upon himself.

And now, can one imagine a brow encountering the world with purest, pristine wonder? Can one see the middle features of a face expressive of unbounded compassion? Can one recognize in the lower part of the face, in the way the jaw is formed, the very embodiment of unswerving conscience—the upholding of the world in all righteousness?

Drawing on these three qualities Rudolf Steiner set out to carve a countenance. It had to transcend anything pertaining to fallen man for Christ was sinless. When Mary Magdalene beheld the Risen One she did not recognize him. She addressed him as the gardener. In the spirit he was not as she had seen him. It was when she heard his voice that she knew him.

Rudolf Steiner connects the mission of the earth with these qualities of wonder, compassion and conscience. The earth has given us the *opportunity* to acquire them and in doing so to become truly human. The countenance, as Rudolf Steiner finally conceived it, transcends the earthly human to become divinely human—a countenance in which nevertheless every human countenance has some part.

The work however went much further, resulting in a carving in wood some thirty feet high, a focal point for the great Goetheanum building then being erected. We can only single out some of the main features to give some idea of what was attempted here.

Commanding the whole and occupying a central place is a figure, more than full size, upright yet in no way static, with the right foot as though stepping forward. In the whole carving Lucifer and Ahriman are twice represented in totally different situations. To the right of the central figure (to the onlooker's left) Lucifer and Ahriman are as though suspended: they appear at first sight to be locked closely together. Lucifer hovers above, with winglike structures billowing over his head, his lower figure dwindling almost to a tail, the end of which curls upwards. Below, Ahriman, his bony wings closely contracted to the sides, with clawlike hands, reaches up as though to grip Lucifer's suspended, up-curling tail. At a casual glance they might seem intimately united, yet in fact they are in bitterest strife. Lucifer, with his

*The Representative of Man*

birdlike, upward-lifting gesture, would seem to scorn the world below, his one intention being to wrest the soul of man away from the earth and carry it off to a kingdom of his own. Ahriman, on the contrary, wishes to mineralize the human body and make it earthbound for ever. Thus the two figures are in a state of arrested strife for possession of the human being, yet there is no space left for him between them. Their apparent interlocking thus conceals their desperate strife. To their left, more greatly proportioned, with forward glance, is the central figure, called by Rudolf Steiner *The Representative of Man*. This figure has his left arm upraised with an inclination leftwards, where we see Lucifer tumbling headlong downwards as from a height above—having, as Rudolf Steiner describes it, broken his own wings in unspeakable agony at beholding 'the true light that lighteth every human being'.

The right arm of that central figure is pointing strongly downwards with an inclination to the right (to our left as we face him) where, sunk below the earth, his wings contracted, his sharp features defiantly looking upwards, we see Ahriman, thrust down as though overwhelmed by the moral force in all its pristine strength which he is obliged to suffer.

There is no trace of tension, of attack or defence, in the central figure, only his presence: in every detail the god of balance between the other two, from above and below, from right to left, even from behind forward as expressed in the advancing right foot, and the countenance expressive of the three qualities described above.

High up on our left, above the interlocked figures, and peeping down as though from behind a parapet, is a third figure observing the drama taking place below, not directly engaged, or not yet.

As we face this carving we are reminded how each one, in the fulfilment of his destiny, must inevitably find himself, not once but many times, somewhere between Lucifer and Ahriman. Awakened to the right quality of wonder he may expel the false light of Lucifer, possessed with a right conscience for truth he may quell the false powers of Ahriman, filled with heart's compassion for the world, he may learn to know his brotherhood in Christ. Nothing imposes on us as onlookers. Only the example stands before us. But we may also realize that human destiny is a stage upon which higher destinies unfold. In this age of freedom, human destiny is raised to a new level, for in so far as we become a conscious participator in shaping the future, acting out of the freedom of our own spirit, we begin to take a new role in the world process. Through the Christ we are raised to a level where we become the youngest hierarchy in the order of creation. Christ said of John the Baptist who ushered in the new age, 'he was the greatest born of woman, yet less than the angels'. And humanity today, finding itself at the dawn of a new age of light, can awaken to what carries it beyond nature to a birth in the spirit. The human being, so far less than the angels, may yet regard himself cosmically as their youngest brother. Steiner's great carving speaks to the very heart of anthroposophy.

But we may ask what is the destiny of beings such as Lucifer and Ahriman. This is the same as asking about the origin of evil, and whether it must be perpetuated. Such questions lead far beyond the scope of this small book, yet there are one or two observations we might make.

Such beings as Lucifer and Ahriman, as we encounter them, appear to have lost all initiative in regard to themselves. They work as natural forces, impervious to appeal. They are obliged to be as they are and to act as they do, always in opposition to the benevolent powers which guide human destiny.

It is through the deed of Lucifer that humanity has sunk more deeply into matter than would otherwise have been the case, and has thereby also fallen prey to Ahriman. The direct effect is our separation in the densified body from the surrounding world. But this is the very precondition, as we have seen, for developing qualities whereby, through the deed of Christ, we can awaken to our own identity upon the path to freedom. In a sense we are indebted to these adverse powers though they for their own part can only act to destroy mankind.

Whereas the good powers hold back, as we have seen, in the case of Michael, and Christ himself, to make room for humanity to realize and advance in freedom, these other powers are ever-insinuating themselves to rob us of our freedom. Rudolf Steiner in his mystery plays gives much evidence of this and how, in the course of development, they have to be met, and above all recognized for what they are.

At the same time, held within the right bounds, they have great gifts for the human being. Lucifer with his upward-lifting nature inspires the impulse to art, to lift life above the commonplace, but if unchecked this can lead to egotism and extravagance. Ahriman is the genius behind technical invention, through which the human being can acquire great conscientiousness and responsibility in handling the physical world. But these qualities if not turned also to inner work give rise to an illusion that the world is nothing but a machine and the human being only a cog in it.

We have to realize that these powers are not only outside us. They are in us and a part of our nature; they are in our blood and nerve. We cannot escape them, we can only transform them so that through humanity, in the far distant future, they may gain some measure of redemption. For example, we little realize the power of our self-love. We can cure ourselves of Lucifer by directing that love away from ourselves and into the world—we can practise increasing our love for the world. We also are coldly indifferent to the things of the world under the mask of objectivity. We can practise turning this objectivity back on ourselves, make use of Ahriman to grow more objectively aware of ourselves.

In this way a more conscious attitude can enter our daily lives beneficially. This brings us back to the early section of this book dealing with exercises. Even such far-reaching considerations can be brought into immediate service.

Yet the adversaries still remain adversaries and will do so for long ages to come, taking a new form with each step in humanity's progress. At this time, at the passage from Kaliyuga into a new age of light, we are sorely beset within and without. It is not only that we confront such perils as are released in atomic energy. The growing bewilderment and increasing helplessness in the world serve as preparation for what has long been foreseen as the advent of a stage of world dictatorship for the extermination of every form of inner freedom, and the creation of every form of unfreedom. Ahriman inspires ingenious machines under the guise of orderly living and Lucifer inspires every form of licence in the name of freedom. The twentieth century has already, in a preliminary way, been a witness of this.

Tragedy and comedy lie deep at the roots of human life and culture. Tragedy is separation, falling apart, becoming lost to one another. Comedy is uniting, meeting again, finding one another. In the great mystery of life every separation over-come leads to a greater meeting. Separation is the price of freedom. Love is the only uniting force. The great gift that mankind is destined to bring into the universe is that of love born of freedom—love in freedom.

If the Antichrist should come, as anthroposophy suggests is inevitable and imminent, the Christ himself is surely there too to reveal himself anew to the human soul. The Antichrist we must learn to recognize, for that defeats him. Christ waits to be received. Our age requires the birth of a heightened consciousness through self-directed endeavour—a new degree of selflessness and service. The way is open. It rests only with the human will.

Who is the Antichrist? This question touches on the deepest secrets of our time. We can only give an indication for further thought and study.

We have entered the age that follows Kali-yuga, an age in which a new spiritual consciousness dawns in humanity, an age whose sustaining strength will be the progressive awakening of mankind to the Risen Christ where he dwells in the etheric world, a world of light and life immediately adjoining the earth. It may also be called the age of the second coming which Christ himself, foretold as described in the Gospels of Matthew, Mark and Luke. He gives warning of false Christs and prophets who will show 'signs and wonders to seduce, if it were possible, even the elect'. He points to a time of great tribulation, fathers against sons and sons against fathers, nation rising against nation and kingdom against kingdom, earthquakes, famines, pestilences, as the 'beginning of sorrows'. There will also be signs in the heavens, in sun, moon and stars. 'And then shall they see the son of man coming in the clouds with great power and glory.'

Rudolf Steiner in 1909 and 1910, and also later, declared that the age of the second advent has indeed begun, that from the 1930s on, first a very few and then gradually more will behold 'Christ in the clouds' or, in anthroposophical language, 'Christ in the etheric' in ways akin to Paul's experience at Damascus, and this will continue until in the space of two thousand five hundred years the whole of humanity will have attained that experience.

It would follow then that the adversaries of whom Christ spoke, whose aim it must be to obscure totally our vision and understanding for the Risen One, will gather up all their opposing strength at this time.

Rudolf Steiner reveals that Lucifer walked the earth in a human body in the third millennium BC. It follows inevitably, therefore, in the course and pattern of history, that Ahriman will similarly be incarnated in the third millennium AD. We would expect him to present himself as a great benefactor, bringing peace and plenty to all but in such a way that every vestige of human freedom will be obliterated. His vast but freezing cold intelligence can only serve the absolute impeccability of the perfect machine. The world is to be his machine, and humanity emptied of heart and soul its crowning piece. We may recognize how much preparation to that end is already underway.

We are in an epoch with Christ in the etheric waiting for humanity to awaken to the full meaning of his words 'I am with you always'; and Ahriman is to appear in outer form on earth as Antichrist to pursue further his work of plunging mankind into uttermost darkness.

When we think of Lucifer incarnated in the ancient East, of Christ in the three years as Jesus of Nazareth from the baptism in the Jordan to the death on the cross, and Ahriman approaching incarnation in the modern West, and see in this a drama of the gods surrounding the human being, we encounter once again the profound significance of the great carving with Christ between Lucifer and Ahriman, and we may begin to grasp why Rudolf Steiner chose to describe that central figure as *The Representative of Man.*

# POSTSCRIPT

The great carving, often referred to as the Group, has a noble space allotted to it high up in the Goetheanum at Dornach, near Basel. It was originally intended for a very different place. Where the Goetheanum now stands, on that same foundation, there once stood another Goetheanum, a totally different building, two-domed, all of wood, a unique structure unlike any other. Rudolf Steiner had designed it in every detail. Many new impulses of art had gone into its inner and outer formation. Ten years of continuous labour went into it. It was spoken of as the House of the Word. Then, in the course of one night, 31 December 1922, it was completely burned down by an act of arson similar to that which burnt down the Temple of Ephesus. Whereas that temple, also dedicated to the Mystery of the Word, was the crowning and last great school of the Greek Mysteries, the first Goetheanum had been conceived to bear witness to the New Mysteries of the present time. The Group was not yet completed and therefore was not in the building, and so, by great good fortune, has been preserved for us.

The destruction of that building, after so much love and devotion had gone into it on the part of many, was a great blow. For Rudolf Steiner, the greatest sorrow was that western eyes in particular would never be able to behold its life-kindling forms.

A year later, during the Christmas week of 1923 leading into New Year's Day 1924, Rudolf Steiner refounded the Anthroposophical Society and gave it a new form. It was to be called the General Anthroposophical Society and all Anthroposophical Societies in different countries throughout the world were to be part of it. The Society was to be open unconditionally to all who had an interest in anthroposophy and its further progress. It was in every sense a 'free' society. In addition, Rudolf Steiner established a School of Spiritual Science for furthering the work of anthroposophy. In connection with it he established a number of 'Sections' to carry particular studies to greater depth and to encourage research.

As a matter of historic interest we list the Sections as they were first founded, and the appointed leaders at the time.

| | |
|---|---|
| The Fine Arts and Literature | Albert Steffen |
| The Performing Arts, Speech, Drama, Eurythmy | Marie Steiner |
| Medicine | Ita Wegman |
| Astronomy and Mathematics | Elizabeth Vreede |
| Science | Guenther Wachsmuth |
| Education | Rudolf Steiner in collaboration with the other Section leaders |

The above named are no longer living but the work represented by the Sections has spread far through the world.

The present Goetheanum was also designed by Rudolf Steiner. He wrote:

For a year I carried about with me the idea for a new Goetheanum. The transformation of this idea, from wood into the artistically brittle substance of concrete, was not easy. Then, at the beginning of this year, I began to work on the model... For many years, in my anthroposophical writings and lectures, I have emphasized the fact that anthroposophy is not only a theoretical conception of the world, but that a special style in art results from its very nature. And, since that is the case, a building for anthroposophy must grow out of this itself...

From the very fact that the second Goetheanum is so very different from the first, we can learn that in spiritual life nothing can be merely repeated. Each fresh endeavour calls for a new deed of creation. This second Goetheanum has inspired many to see how forms in space, entering the eye, can quicken an experience of awakening in the beholder.

The burning of the first Goetheanum had, from all accounts, deprived Rudolf Steiner of much strength. In the period following the establishment of the General Anthroposophical Society, his physical strength was depleted still further, yet never had he worked so hard as in the months that followed.

Marie Steiner, his wife, writes about this period:

Every day, three courses revealing an inexpressible power of spiritual ascent. In addition at least three lectures every week about anthroposophy and magnificent lectures for those working on the building. One dared not utter a word about sparing him. Pleas to spare himself constituted a hindrance.

She also writes that 'The doorkeepers counted four hundred visitors during the time when he was giving four lectures each day.'

In June 1924, at the request of farmers Steiner inaugurated a new method of agriculture now widely known and practised as biodynamic agriculture.

In August 1924 he made his last visit to England, and amongst much else gave a lecture course on education as basis for the first English Waldorf School based on the Waldorf School in Stuttgart which he himself had founded in 1919.

On 28 September 1924, the eve of Michaelmas, he gave his last lecture. He did not appear in public again.

Dr Wachsmuth, who was his daily attendant and messenger at this time, writes:

Lying in his room, he loved the living noise of hammering and scaffold-building which penetrated from the building site of the Goetheanum into the quiet of his sickroom, announcing the birth of the building.

But he did not live to see it.

Each week he sent in a handwritten article for members dealing with one aspect or another of Michael's battle on behalf of humanity, now with Lucifer, now with Ahriman, and always in intimate connection with the Christ—a marvellous concentration of material for study and for meditative work.

But, according to Dr Wachsmuth who had to supply him with these things, 'he also did a tremendous amount of reading, keeping himself continuously informed of literature newly published in all fields including science, art and history'.

He died on the thirtieth day of March, 1925.

Dr Wachsmuth wrote:

The forward-striding figure of the Christ statue, pointing into the expanses of the universe, which he himself had created and at whose feet he now lay, spoke for the eyes of those left behind on the earth of what was here taking place for the spirit of a great human being, who had dedicated his life to annunciation of the Christ.

The work he initiated in so many fields has continued to grow and expand and has reached all lands where a free spiritual and cultural life is possible.

The development of Rudolf Steiner's anthroposophical work covers a relatively short period of time, 1902–25. It ranges from great cosmic conceptions to a deep engagement in the arts, leading on to a detailed consideration of many practical fields of work. Beholding the human being in the light of all this, one could truly say that this work embodies the full potential and ideal of humanity.

The cosmic aspect of anthroposophy not only includes descriptions of the hierarchical beings directly concerned with human and world evolution, but also offers a basis for the study of the heavenly bodies, stars, sun, moon and planets in their present influences on nature and the human being. This has proved greatly enlightening for practising teachers, doctors and farmers.

What came strongly to expression in the arts was the principle of metamorphosis, of organic progress and transformation. This was clearly to be seen in the architecture, sculpture and the painting of the first Goetheanum. All these three arts received new impulses, raising an underlying creative principle in nature to new modes of realization through the human being. The mystery plays made similar demands for a new art of theatre as regards speech, dramatic gesture, music, colour and form. Speech formation was developed as a new art of recitation.

A special mention can be made here of eurythmy, a new art of movement initiated by Rudolf Steiner, described also as visible speech and visible song. It is an art in which motion and gesture have their origin in the primordial sources of the elements of language and of music which engendered the human form. It can therefore translate itself with equal immediacy into every language and mode of music. In this art, light and colour also play a great part.

In the last years, from 1917 on, anthroposophy reached ever more practical spheres of daily life: medicine, including cancer research, and the production of a new range of medicaments, mainly homoeopathic, for internal and external treatment; a new art of education, more generally known as Waldorf education, and, as a parallel but independent development, curative education; a new science of agriculture (biodynamics) which, as well as being the precursor of the organic farming movement, also engages planetary and zodiac constellation forces to enhance soil fertility; and research in mathematics and in various scientific fields.

In addition to all else, in response to a request from a number of pastors, he conducted special studies with them and later enabled them, on their own responsibility, to found the church of the Christian Community for the renewal of religious life based on a renewed understanding of the sacraments.

All this activity unfolded in the first quarter of this century, contributing to the emergence, out of our materialistic times, of a new era of culture, well schooled in the disciplines of scientific method and observation, but also including the supersensible realities of human existence. Anthroposophy thus goes far beyond a conception of the world and the cosmos to become a *way of life* that fully penetrates all aspects of our everyday existence in will, feeling and thought, and in every practical sphere of work.

# AFTERWORD

Since Francis Edmunds died in 1989, the world has of course moved on considerably, as has the anthroposophical movement. Edmunds's fundamental insights into the nature of anthroposophy remain as valid today as when he wrote this book, but the fields of work drawing inspiration from it have developed and diversified, and continue to seek fruitful interaction with the realities and problems of the modern world. The list below, of current work that draws inspiration from anthroposophy, is not an exhaustive one, but may give a sense of the great diversity of such work, and the rich source which anthroposophy continues to be.

## *Education*

New Rudolf Steiner or Waldorf schools continue to open throughout the world, adapting to the specific cultural context of each country and offering a counterbalance to one-sided educational provision—whether accentuating 'head' (highly academic education) or 'limbs' (specialized practical training geared to specific socio-economic tasks). Steiner education does not deny the validity of either of these poles, but seeks to balance them in a heartfelt way, combining intellect and practical activity in an artistic whole that addresses the essential being of every child.

Increasing internationalism and pluralism in the Waldorf school movement has led to collaboration with bodies such as Unesco, and support of Steiner schools in developing countries. At the same time links are being forged with related initiatives, such as the European Forum for Freedom in

Education (EFFE) and, since 1999, the 'Alliance for Childhood'. Worldwide there are currently 875 schools and 1500 early years centres in 60 countries, and 60 teacher training centres.

## *Special needs education and social therapy*

Likewise an international movement, anthroposophical special needs or curative education, has now spread to 40 countries on all continents, with regular international conferences and mutual support networks aimed at nurturing children and adults with special needs and recognizing their full humanity. Currently the focus is on establishing day schools and integrative institutions for children, and on creating sheltered living and work facilities for adults. Anthroposophical special needs education has become an acknowledged part of the social provision network in many countries, but often must fight hard to assert its profoundly human approach against increasingly strict state guidelines and restrictions.

## *Medicine*

Anthroposophical medicine is an integrative approach that draws both on the huge range of knowledge and methods available in mainstream medicine but also, at the same time, on spiritual science. It differs from purely orthodox medicine in its perception that human beings are more than their physical bodies, consisting also of a non-material soul and individuality. It does not view itself as an 'alternative' medicine but one which extends the mainstream perspective to take account of each human being's unique qualities. Every treatment should therefore respect this uniqueness, as expressed, for instance, in a patient's physical gestures, biography, breathing and much more. The anthroposophical doctor seeks the patient's active involvement in the healing process, in therapies ranging from painting, music, modelling and movement therapies through to rhythmic massage, diet and biography work. Anthroposophical medicines vary from whole plant extracts to homoeopathic remedies, and seek to activate a patient's own self-healing capacities. However allopathic medicines are also used where necessary. Recent developments include an internationally acknowledged therapy programme for addicts, and a wide range of new research projects to prove the efficacy of remedies such as mistletoe in treating cancer. Anthroposophical medicines are legally recognized in six EU states, and legislative initiatives are underway in other countries to secure recognition. The Council of Europe's 1999 resolution no. 1206 ('A European Approach to Non-Conventional Medicines') singles out anthroposophical medicine as significant.

## Biodynamic agriculture and nutrition

Besides rejecting artificial fertilizers and pesticides, the work of biodynamic farmers and growers is also based on appropriate crop rotation, animal husbandry in keeping with animals' needs, and efforts to enliven the earth and its plants through biodynamic preparations derived from medicinal herbs, cow-dung, and specific minerals. Each farm, as a complete organism, strives to attain a harmonious unity between human beings, animals and plants, and also takes cosmic moon and zodiac rhythms into account. Over the years many biodynamic research centres have carried out studies to show the effectiveness of this form of agriculture—such as the Biochemical Research Laboratory in Spring

Valley, USA, and the Louis-Bolk Institute in Holland. The latter has been at the forefront of studies on questions of gene technology; and the biodynamic movement has actively combated the introduction of genetically engineered crops, for instance in a 2003 memorandum, signed by over 5000 people, highlighting the impossibility of coexistence between organic and genetic technology farming methods. Demeter International now actively engages with European agriculture policy in Brussels, focusing on foodstuff quality and arguing against industrial agricultural methods. Biodynamic produce and wines have been awarded many top prizes for quality, taste and positive impact on the environment. The first chair of biodynamic agriculture was established at Kassel University in 2005, and this farming method is now being used on over 3000 farms in thirty-five countries.

## Science

Anthroposophical spiritual science does not conflict with modern science but strives to deepen and extend it. Founded on the scientific explorations and methods of Goethe it practises a holistic approach involving accurate observation of material phenomena but at the same time seeking the spiritual realities that underlie them. Along these lines the anthroposophical scientist tries to discover the living unity linking a wide diversity of phenomena. Research drawing on Goethe's approach, but also taking full account of modern scientific testing and methodology, is currently being done in the fields of biology, evolution, geology, chemistry and physics, and also in more applied fields such as ecology, agriculture, pharmacy, quality research, and water purification and revitalization through natural rhythms. Scientists working in these and related fields have published large amounts of research, some of which has received attention in mainstream journals such as *Nature*.

## Social sciences

The Goetheanum's Section for Social Sciences acts as coordinating centre for a wide network of projects throughout the world that aim to develop new social forms and provide a counterbalance to some of the ills affecting human society. Based on Steiner's research these diverse projects range from conflict resolution in companies or communities through to work in the political and economic field and ethical banking. One of Steiner's fundamental ideas about society was that economic factors should not dictate and control other spheres of life such as those of culture and human rights—a phenomenon that has increased drastically as vast multinationals have come to exert as much political and financial power as governments or whole nations. One ongoing project based on anthroposophy is the so-called Economics Conference, an international group that meets at least once each year as a forum for independent researchers to share their work and develop insights based on spiritual science into the problems of economic life.

## Religion

Founded in 1922 as a 'movement for religious renewal', the Christian Community aims to reinvigorate Christianity and religious life through new sacraments and services based on the spiritual insights of anthroposophy. Its core service, the 'Act of Consecration of Man' reflects a path of development through Gospel teaching, sacrifice, transformation and communion. The Christian Community regards the deed of

Christ as the central, decisive event in world history, giving an upward direction to evolution once more and safeguarding humanity from losing its spiritual connection in an ever-deepening descent into matter. Priests undergo thorough training at one of the Christian Community training centres (Germany and America), pursuing studies in a very wide range of practical, artistic and theoretical fields. The religious dimension of anthroposophy is absolutely opposed to all sectarianism, and fully recognizes the unique and valid contribution of each religion to human evolution.

## The arts

Anthroposophy sees the arts as arising from human beings' free endeavour and intuition, and thus there is no such thing as 'anthroposophical art'. But anthroposophy does enrich and stimulate a wide range of artistic fields.

*Architecture:* Steiner pioneered highly original organic architecture, designing many buildings himself including the first and second Goetheanum. During the twentieth century many architects from all continents drew on this source of inspiration. They tried to develop an architecture that is in tune with the times and human needs, and in which a building's inherent function is expressed artistically in its outer form and inner dimensions.

*Sculpture, painting:* The development of anthroposophically inspired sculpture was closely related to the first Goetheanum building, almost all of whose interior was sculpted in wood. Anthroposophically inspired sculpture and painting are preoccupied as much with the laws and lawfulness inherent in their materials (stone, clay or colour etc.) and in the cosmos, as with personal expression of emotion or idea. The anthroposophical art scene is very lively and highly diverse, and many artists pursue their own, very different styles. One very well-known twentieth-century artist inspired by Steiner was Joseph Beuys, an exhibition of whose work is currently being held at Tate Modern in London. Beuys pioneered a very original social dimension to art in his 'actions', and was preoccupied with art as a spiritual force in everyday life.

*Poetry, speech, drama and storytelling:* Here again there are a wide range of different groups and individuals exploring and experimenting in diverse ways, but all drawing in some way on Steiner's insights and suggestions. A common preoccupation in all these fields is the attempt to make language—whether on the page or orally—into a vehicle for the spirit, and to explore and express the hidden wealth inherent in language as something that requires continual effort and renewal. In modern technological culture language so easily hardens into fixed, inflexible forms, becoming a straitjacket rather than a living, breathing vessel. Poetry and drama can question and counter this.

*Music:* Steiner was aware that the classical and romantic era marked the end of an epoch, and that from the beginning of the twentieth century onwards mighty changes were afoot. Such changes demanded and continue to demand a new preoccupation with the fundamental elements of music, the quality of the single tone and exploration of new intervals. Music and singing inspired by anthroposophy seeks to penetrate the qualities and forces at work in tones and intervals so as to give expression to cosmic and spiritual dimensions of experience. Numerous composers and musicians have drawn on this sphere of musical work, whether in the areas of new instrument building, composing, music therapy or education. Viktor Ullmann, a musician inspired by anthroposophy who composed operas during his imprisonment in concentration camps and died during the Holocaust, has received wide attention recently.

*Eurythmy:* This new art of movement developed by Steiner aims to reveal the laws and dynamics inherent in speech and music through the medium of bodily gesture and to incorporate these into an artistic flow—unlike most other dance forms which accompany word or music with interpretative movements. Stage eurythmy has changed, developed and diversified through the years, but even in the most modern garb it seeks to draw on this spiritual source. Eurythmy therapy is widely and successfully used for a large number of complaints, and supports anthroposophical medicines in activating the body's self-healing forces.

MATTHEW BARTON
2005

*Steiner*

## A NOTE FROM RUDOLF STEINER PRESS

We are an independent publisher and registered charity (non-profit organisation) dedicated to making available the work of Rudolf Steiner in English translation. We care a great deal about the content of our books and have hundreds of titles available – as printed books, ebooks and in audio formats.

## As a publisher devoted to anthroposophy...

- We continually commission translations of previously unpublished works by Rudolf Steiner and invest in re-translating, editing and improving our editions.

- We are committed to making anthroposophy available to all by publishing introductory books as well as contemporary research.

- Our new print editions and ebooks are carefully checked and proofread for accuracy, and converted into all formats for all platforms.

- Our translations are officially authorised by Rudolf Steiner's estate in Dornach, Switzerland, to whom we pay royalties on sales, thus assisting their critical work.

So, look out for Rudolf Steiner Press as a mark of quality and support us today by buying our books, or contact us should you wish to sponsor specific titles or to support the charity with a gift or legacy.

office@rudolfsteinerpress.com
Join our e-mailing list at www.rudolfsteinerpress.com

## RUDOLF STEINER PRESS